ESSENTIALS
for
LIFE

Your Back-to-Basics Guide to What Matters Most

Marcia Ford

THOMAS NELSON
Since 1798

NASHVILLE   DALLAS   MEXICO CITY   RIO DE JANEIRO

Published in Nashville, Tennessee, by Thomas Nelson. Thomas Nelson is a registered trademark of Thomas Nelson, Inc.

Thomas Nelson, Inc., titles may be purchased in bulk for educational, business, fund-raising, or sales promotional use. For information, please e-mail SpecialMarkets@ThomasNelson.com.

Scripture quotations noted AMP are from THE AMPLIFIED BIBLE: Old Testament. © 1962, 1964 by Zondervan Publishing House (used by permission); and from THE AMPLIFIED NEW TESTAMENT. © 1958 by the Lockman Foundation (used by permission).

Scripture quotations noted NIV are from the HOLY BIBLE: NEW INTERNATIONAL VERSION®. © 1973,1978,1984 by International Bible Society. Used by permission of Zondervan Publishing House. All rights reserved.

Scripture quotations noted MSG are from THE MESSAGE by Eugene H. Peterson. © 1993, 1994, 1995, 1996, 2000, 2001, 2002. Used by permission of NavPress Publishing Group.

Scripture quotations NLT are from the Holy Bible, New Living Translation, © 1996, 2004. Used by permission of Tyndale House Publishers, Inc., Wheaton, Illinois 60189. All rights reserved.

Scripture quotations noted NASB are from the NEW AMERICAN STANDARD BIBLE®. © The Lockman Foundation 1960, 1962, 1963, 1968, 1971, 1972, 1973, 1975, 1977, 1995. Used by permission.

Scripture quotations noted NCV are from The Holy Bible, New Century Version, © 2005 by Thomas Nelson, Inc. All rights reserved. Used by permission.

Scripture quotations noted NKJV are from THE NEW KING JAMES VERSION. © 1979, 1980, 1982 by Thomas Nelson, Inc., Publishers.

Library of Congress Control Number: 2009938765

ISBN 978-0-7852-2968-1

Editor: Lila Empson Wavering
Associate Editor: Jenn McNeil
Design: Whisner Design Group

Printed in the United States of America

10 11 12 13 14 WC 9 8 7 6 5 4 3 2

You can be sure that God will take care of everything you need, his generosity exceeding even yours in the glory that pours from Jesus. Our God and Father abounds in glory that just pours out into eternity. Yes.

Philippians 4:19–20 MSG

ESSENTIALS *for* LIFE
Contents

apply your beliefs to the way you live reveals your understanding of what faith is.

Fascination with the afterlife results in a great deal of speculation. Christians do not need to speculate, however. Christians have a window to eternity right in the New Testament.

Jesus told his followers to preach the gospel to the entire world. Are you convinced he was talking to you?

Putting together all that you believe about God and his purpose for humankind and applying it to the way you perceive the relationship between the church and culture helps to form a distinctly biblical worldview.

This is it—step number one in your effort to draw closer to God. By committing your life to Jesus, you open yourself up to all that God has for you.

The Bible is the gateway to understanding who God is and the plan he had for humanity since before the beginning of time.

When you allow portions of Scripture to seep into your spirit, you build up a stockpile of wisdom that is available to you just when you need it.

Finding time to spend alone with God may be challenging in a twenty-four/seven culture, but it is not impossible. Planning that time is the key.

With every situation in which you trust God no matter what, you grow closer to him and learn more about the way he wants to work in your life.

they took the time to pay attention to the things that bring them renewed energy and joy.

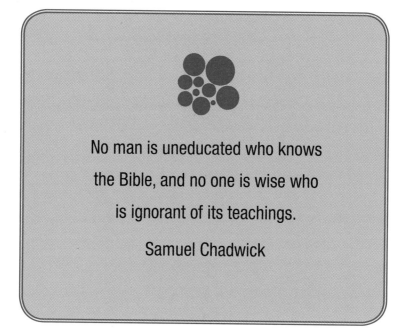

No man is uneducated who knows
the Bible, and no one is wise who
is ignorant of its teachings.

Samuel Chadwick

Introduction

What is actually essential to your life—the well-being of your body, your mind, your spirit?

Answering that question may seem like a daunting task. After all, the word *essential* can cover a lot of territory, from your need for love to your need for a full tank of gas in your car. The best way to navigate that territory is to distill the essentials to a manageable scope and number.

That is what you will find in the pages that follow—a distillation of the essentials to fifty dimensions of life. Reducing all the important aspects of life to only fifty topics is, of course, impossible. These essentials are not intended to offer the final word on the crucial issues of life, but they cover ground that people of faith recognize as vital to a full and fruitful life with God and other people.

Each essential draws on the wisdom found in the Bible to help you think deeply about the topic at hand. The idea is to help you examine your own life in that area and determine for yourself if

Even if it was written in Scripture long ago, you can be sure it's written for us. God wants the combination of his steady, constant calling and warm, personal counsel in Scripture to come to characterize us, keeping us alert for whatever he will do next.

Romans 15:4 MSG

you need to make some adjustments in order to experience that "full and fruitful" existence.

If you are feeling overwhelmed by both a cluttered house and a cluttered schedule, for example, "Simplify Your Lifestyle" may help you think differently about what is essential to your sense of well-being. Likewise, if you have this nagging feeling that you need to try to mend a rift between you and a friend who offended you, "Learn to Forgive" may help you gain a fresh perspective on the situation.

In addition to biblical wisdom, the thoughts of people from a wide variety of experiences and backgrounds are included to help you see life from diverse viewpoints. Whether you agree with the sentiments expressed in the quotations is not as important as their value in helping you to clarify your own viewpoint on the topics.

Some essentials will likely be more relevant to your life right now than others are. But do not neglect the others—in them you may find the wisdom for the future to help a loved one for whom the topic is relevant.

What Do I Believe?

Do good to your servant according to your word, O LORD. Teach me knowledge and good judgment, for I believe in your commands. Before I was afflicted I went astray, but now I obey your word.

Psalm 119:65–67 NIV

Faith is not so much belief about God as it is total, personal trust in God, rising to a personal fellowship with God that is stronger than anxiety and guilt, loneliness and all manner of disaster.

Frederick Ward Kates

Faith says not, "I see that it is good for me, so God must have sent it," but, "God sent it, and so it must be good for me."

Phillips Brooks

Answer the Big Question

For millennia, theologians and philosophers have debated the meaning of life. Today, questions about the meaning of life are explored on YouTube and condensed to 140 characters on Twitter. While you need to keep your finger on that pulse of the bigger debate, here is an equally important question: what is the meaning of your life?

Whether you want to discover the meaning of Life with a capital *L* or the purpose of your own life, it makes sense to go to the Creator of life for the answer. And where better to seek his purpose than the Bible?

But that poses a problem. No sooner do you read in Genesis 1 that humanity was created to populate the earth and have authority over it than someone objects to that conclusion. No, they will tell you, keep reading! Later on the Bible states, "Now all has been heard; here is the conclusion of the matter: Fear God and keep his commandments, for this is the whole duty of man" (Ecclesiastes 12:13 NIV).

In Him also we have obtained an inheritance, being predestined according to the purpose of Him who works all things according to the counsel of His will, that we who first trusted in Christ should be to the praise of His glory.

Ephesians 1:11–12 NKJV

If God exists and we are made in his image we can have real meaning, and we can have real knowledge through what he has communicated to us.

Francis Schaeffer

But wait. Jesus said that people were put here to love God and their neighbor (Matthew 22:37–39) and to preach the gospel to everyone (Matthew 28:19–20).

The point is that life cannot be reduced to one meaning. Life as God intended it is rich with many meanings—plural. And while some people may discover the overarching purpose of their lives—such as Billy Graham's indisputable evangelistic purpose—you can be content by realizing that simply because you are a child of God, your life has profound meaning and a myriad of purposes.

Life isn't like a book. Life isn't logical or sensible or orderly. Life is a mess most of the time. And theology must be lived in the midst of that mess.
—Charles Caleb Colton

But maybe you do not feel that way right now. Maybe it seems as if nothing has ever really worked out for you. Or maybe you once had it all and now feel like a failure because you have lost it all. Trying to convince you that your life has meaning and purpose is pointless. Even your relationship with God, which was once so vibrant and exciting, could now be on the wane.

Before you despair that not even Life with a capital *L* has meaning—let alone your own—take a deep breath and open your Bible to the book of Ecclesiastes. It is not particularly long, but reading it in a modern paraphrase or modern language version like *The Message* or *New Living Translation* may hold your interest better. In Ecclesiastes you will find the writings of a

Never before have people dealt with as many profound issues as they do today, with beginning-of-life and end-of-life questions being asked of people who must make serious decisions. Clarifying your thinking on the meaning of life ahead of time will help if you find yourself in that position.

We are His workmanship, created in Christ Jesus for good works, which God prepared beforehand that we should walk in them.

Ephesians 2:10 NKJV

man who also despaired of the meaning of life. But what he discovered in the process of reflecting on life was that while much of life is absurd, fleeting, and futile, a life that belongs to God is a life worth living. (If your Bible has a section in it called Apocrypha or Deuterocanonicals, you will find a book there called Ecclesiasticus. That is an entirely different book.)

You are not on earth by accident. Your life was intentional and created by God with a purpose. Like everyone else who ever lived, you are here because it pleased God to create you. The entire Bible reflects that purpose; these verses affirm it:

- "You are worthy, O Lord our God, to receive glory and honor and power. For you created all things, and they exist because you created what you pleased" (Revelation 4:11 NLT).

- "The LORD takes pleasure in His people; He will beautify the afflicted ones with salvation" (Psalm 149:4 NASB).

- "He predestined us to be adopted as his sons through Jesus Christ, in accordance with his pleasure and will" (Ephesians 1:5 NIV).

Do not be afraid to ask God about all this. Ask him why you are here, why he created you, what meaning your life could possibly have. Wait for his answer; expect an answer from him. If you start to question whether he had a purpose in creating you, read Psalm 139. Even better, memorize Psalm 139 so it will be fresh in your mind and heart anytime you begin to doubt that God actually wanted you to be born.

what's essential

Whether you can see it or not, God has assured you that he has not cut you adrift. He intends to see your purpose fulfilled, "for it is God who is at work in you, both to will and to work for His good pleasure" (Philippians 2:13 NASB).

DO remind yourself—or better yet, ask God to remind you—of the positive influence you have had on other people.

DO read the Scriptures with the meaning of your life in mind.

DON'T waste precious time despairing of the meaning of life; instead, enjoy the one life you've been given.

DON'T fall prey to the philosophy that all of life is absurd; your life with God is not.

Refine Your Image of God

Everyone has an image of God. Whether it is a visual depiction or an abstract concept, that image affects the way a person relates to God, trusts God, and presents God to others. What is your image of God? If you have not ever thought about it, your image of God may need to be freshened up a bit.

In 2006, a team of professors at Baylor University in Waco, Texas, conducted a survey of religious beliefs in America. One unexpected finding showed that Americans' images of God fit neatly into four categories: authoritarian, benevolent, distant, and critical. From those four images, researchers were able to predict with an impressive degree of accuracy the individual respondent's gender, income level, and political affiliation.

A description of God that can fit that neatly into a group of survey questions is not likely to present a complete picture of how an individual sees God. Imagine that you were one of the respondents; could your image of God be accurately captured on a survey form? The reality is that no two people are likely to have an identical image of who God is, because so many factors—many of them highly personal—combine to create that image.

Think about the people who first taught you about God, whether directly or indirectly. Was it a loving parent, an influential Sunday school teacher—or a cranky neighbor who had no use for God or the church? Many children grow up with conflicting ideas about God, impressions they have to overcome as they enter adulthood and their faith matures. The classic example is that of an adult who as a child was brutally abused by his or her father or a father figure; seeing God as a loving father may prove to be an insurmountable obstacle in such cases.

 God is not a power or principle or law, but he is a living, creating, communicating person—a mind who thinks, a heart who feels, a will who acts, whose best name is Father.
—Robert Hamill

If your image of God has never matured—or has not matured much—beyond the way you thought of him as a child, it is time to give that image a transformation. The way you see God determines the way you relate to him, and the way you relate to him is an essential factor in the way you live out your faith. If you see God as a distant, stern taskmaster who criticizes every little thing you do, you will approach God in a dramatically different way from someone who sees God as a kind of Santa Claus, cheerfully handing out gifts to good little children.

A good place to start this process of transforming your image of God is the Bible. The Bible offers these depictions of God, among many others:

- Mother comforting her son (Isaiah 66:13)

- Fortress and a refuge (Psalm 91:2)

- Light and salvation (Psalm 27:1)

- Shepherd (Psalm 23)

- Rock and a stronghold (Psalm 62:2)

- Love (1 John 4:16)

- Potter (Jeremiah 18:6)

- Vine (John 15:5)

Sometimes, all it takes to shake up a person's image of God is a few choice words from someone who looks at God through an entirely different lens—someone like G. K. Chesterton, who got to thinking one day about how little children seldom tire of repetition: "It is possible that God says every morning, 'Do it again' to the sun; and every evening, 'Do it again' to the moon. It may not be automatic necessity that makes all daisies alike; it may be that God makes every daisy separately, but has never got tired of making them. It may be that He has the eternal appetite of infancy."

God is not a man, that He should lie, nor a son of man, that He should repent. Has He said, and will He not do? Or has He spoken, and will He not make it good?

Numbers 23:19 NKJV

Can you imagine God being younger than you? Chesterton did. Your image of God is limited only by your Spirit-controlled imagination and the portrayals of God in the Bible. Shake things up a bit—and release God from the box you have been keeping him in.

what's essential

If your image of God is flawed or immature, your relationship with him will likewise be flawed and immature. If you have a mature understanding of who God is, you are more likely to enjoy a healthy relationship with God that is free of faulty impressions left over from your childhood.

DO search the Scriptures to discover what the Bible has to say about who God is.

DO spend focused time on refining your image of God.

DON'T be afraid to examine images of God that you have not considered before.

DON'T make the mistake of fashioning God in your image; you were made in his image and not vice versa.

Seek the Truth About Jesus

Studies questioning the divinity of Jesus have long been a staple in religious and academic circles. But in recent years, news-magazines, outspoken atheists, and books and movies such as The Da Vinci Code *have brought the debate into the mainstream. So just who was—or is—Jesus? And what do you believe about him?*

Ever since Jesus' earthly ministry, people have tried to reduce him to something he is not by ob-scuring the truth about who he is. He was just a wise teacher, they say, or maybe one of many prophets of God. It is true that "wise teacher" and "prophet" are accurate descriptors, as far as they go. But Christians believe that Jesus was not just anything; he is everything and always will be.

Many Christians readily accept the biblical nar-rative about Jesus without question, study, or close examination. Their lives and ways of think-ing have been so transformed that they need no more convincing. Jesus is the Son of God, plain and simple. Nothing short of a genuine miracle could account for the dramatic change that their faith in Jesus has made in their lives.

If a man fights his way through his doubts to the conviction that Jesus Christ is Lord, he has attained to a certainty that the man who unthinkingly accepts things can never reach.

William Barclay

Other people, though, are not so sure. Without a doubt, they say, Jesus was a unique individual. He was loving, wise, and compassionate. And he was courageous; no one stood up to Pharisees the way he did. But the risen Messiah, the Son of God? Not so fast. He was simply an extraordinary human being who lived and died like everyone else, and probably fathered a child with Mary Magdalene, who may or may not have been his wife, as any number of novels and nonfiction books have suggested. His disciples made up the empty-tomb story along with accounts of his post-crucifixion appearances. They needed a life-size god; Jesus fit the bill.

 Jesus' good news, then, was that the Kingdom of God had come, and that he, Jesus, was its herald and expounder to men. More than that, in some special and mysterious way, he was the kingdom.
—Malcolm Muggeridge

How about you? Do you believe Jesus is the resurrected Son of God, the third person of the Trinity, the Savior? Or do you believe he is one of many prophets? Maybe your understanding of who he is lies somewhere in between; maybe you see him as one of many gods, with a lowercase *g*.

The thing about Jesus, however, is that he left no room in the middle. Jesus is either the Son of God as he claimed to be, or he isn't, in which case he is a fraud and hardly worth calling a wise teacher or prophet. Likewise, neither the Scriptures nor the apostles are trustworthy, proclaiming as they did that Jesus was the resurrected Savior of the world.

If you are not clear on who Jesus is, seek the truth about him. Search the Scriptures and examine the arguments against his divinity. And then search your heart. Decide for yourself who Jesus is, because until you personally settle that question, your relationship with God will be incomplete and based on doubt rather than faith. Here are some Scriptures to use to start your search:

- Jesus himself claimed to be God (John 8:24–29, 56–59; 10:30–33).

- Others called him God (John 1:1, 1:14; 20:28; Colossians 2:9; Titus 2:13; Hebrews 1:8).

- As God, Jesus created everything (John 1:3; Colossians 1:15–17).

- Jesus is with people today (Matthew 18:20; 28:20).

- Jesus lives forever (Micah 5:2; Hebrews 7:24).

- Jesus has the power to forgive sins (Matthew 9:1–7; Luke 5:20; 7:48).

A good concordance or topical Bible, both of which can be found online, can direct you to dozens of other Bible verses that affirm Jesus' divinity. As you are searching, also look at the behavior of

Christ's followers after their discovery of the empty tomb. Look, too, at the growth of the early church, the sacrifices made by early believers, and the danger they placed themselves in. Their actions speak of people whose lives had been transformed by a supernatural power.

When you are ready to conclude who Jesus is, remember this: what you believe about him is nothing short of life-changing.

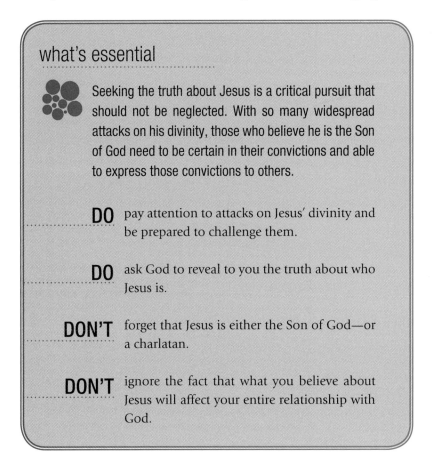

what's essential

Seeking the truth about Jesus is a critical pursuit that should not be neglected. With so many widespread attacks on his divinity, those who believe he is the Son of God need to be certain in their convictions and able to express those convictions to others.

DO pay attention to attacks on Jesus' divinity and be prepared to challenge them.

DO ask God to reveal to you the truth about who Jesus is.

DON'T forget that Jesus is either the Son of God—or a charlatan.

DON'T ignore the fact that what you believe about Jesus will affect your entire relationship with God.

Grasp the Resurrection's Impact

I am the Living One;
I was dead, and behold
I am alive for ever and
ever! And I hold the keys
of death and Hades.

Revelation 1:18 NIV

Have you ever wondered about the resurrection—how it happened, why it happened, if it happened? How about this: have you ever wondered how different your life would be had the resurrection never occurred? There is no doubt about that one. Your life would be dramatically different.

Most people, even Christians, probably do not give a lot of thought to the resurrection except at Easter. As an object of meditation, the crucifixion, or more specifically, the suffering Jesus endured on the cross, almost certainly surpasses the resurrection. Most Christians, of course, fully understand the impact of the resurrection but probably do not think about how it affects their everyday lives.

It is, of course, impossible to exaggerate the importance of the historicity of what is commonly known as the Resurrection. If, after all His claims and promises, Christ had died and merely lived on as a fragrant memory, He would only be revered as an extremely good but profoundly mistaken man.

J. B. Phillips

But think about it now. Stop and consider what your everyday life would be like if Jesus had not risen from the dead. It is close to impossible to imagine it, really. If Jesus had died like everyone else, remaining in the grave, you would have no church, no salvation, no Savior to believe in—at least, not the true Savior. Civilization as you know it would simply not exist.

That is a lot to take in, but it is all true. The resurrection of Jesus set in motion the future course of world events. Because he was raised from the dead, his followers shouted the news from the rooftops and established a body of believers who not only became a saving influence in countless lives but also became a cultural influence in every sphere of life.

As important as all that is, focus for a few minutes on your own life and how the resurrection affects you today, starting with those first few days after the crucifixion.

 When Jesus Christ shed his blood on the cross, it was not the blood of a martyr; or the blood of one man for another; it was the life of God poured out to redeem the world.
—Oswald Chambers

If Jesus' disciples had not found an empty tomb when they went to prepare his body for burial—if his body had been there and had later been buried—his followers would have faded into obscurity. Many were already in hiding, afraid of being associated with this man who had just been crucified like a common criminal. At best, Christianity would have ended up as a cult populated by a few true believers; at worst, there would have been nothing resembling a religious movement with Jesus as its leader. No resurrection, no church for you.

If Jesus had not been raised from the dead, and had he not proven that fact by appearing to his followers numerous times before his ascension into heaven, his death on the cross would have been futile. Only by dying and returning to life could Jesus prove that he was indeed the Son of God and that he had authority over life and death, in heaven and on earth. His death on the cross—his sacrificial death for the sins of the world—would have been meaningless. No resurrection, no salvation for you.

Finally, Jesus' resurrection offered tangible hope for the resurrection of believers. Through his resurrection, he proved he had victory over death—not just for himself but for all his followers. For the first time in human history, people began to view death as transition and not finality. Believers could spend eternity in the presence of God! This was, and still is, astonishing news, but it could be accomplished only if Jesus paved the way by being raised from the dead. No resurrection, no eternal life for you.

Recognizing the significance of the resurrection is critical to both your present faith and your future hope. Without it, you have no basis on which to place your salvation or your hope of spending eternity with God. Far from being simply a pleas-

ant concept and a reason to celebrate on Easter Sunday, the resurrection is a dramatic, historical event that changed the course
of history and whose impact resonated down through the centuries to where you are today. Through it, Jesus conquered death—
he conquered death!—for all who believe in him.

what's essential

The resurrection is foundational to your belief in Jesus as the Son of God. Deny the resurrection, and you may as well deny the entire basis for your faith in God. Belief in the bodily resurrection of Christ is as essential to your faith as any other belief you hold.

DO spend time reflecting on the resurrection and the impact it has had on your own life.

DO read the accounts of Jesus' postresurrection appearances, which revealed him to be a physical person and not an apparition.

DON'T fall for the teaching that alleges the accounts of Jesus' resurrection were fabricated by his followers.

DON'T forget that Jesus' followers placed their lives on the line after the resurrection, something they would not have done had Jesus not proven himself to be the true Son of God.

Know Who the Spirit Is

If you like a classic mystery, you need look no further than the Bible for some great material. God has revealed much of the story, but some things remain a mystery— like a full understanding of the Trinity. Despite everything known about the third member of the Trinity, some people are still confused about who the Holy Spirit is.

Some aspects of Christianity are known as *mysteries*, a term used in the New Testament to describe concepts such as the incarnation that cannot be fully comprehended this side of heaven. Unlike fictional mysteries, religious mysteries cannot be neatly wrapped up at the end of a book or movie. You will have to be content knowing that you will not know it all until you come face-to-face with God.

One such mystery is the Trinity, the doctrine that defines the three-in-one nature of God— God the Father, God the Son, and God the Holy Spirit—one God in three persons or personalities. Within the Godhead, the Holy Spirit is the least understood and the most misrepresented. While the Trinity may remain a mystery, there is no reason why the Holy Spirit should. The Bible tells us so much about the Spirit that when it comes to evidence of God's activity in the lives of believers on earth, it is clear who is responsible: the Holy Spirit.

To understand the Holy Spirit, however, you need to start from the right foundation, which is this: the Holy Spirit is a person. The Spirit is not some impersonal force in the universe that serves as a source of spiritual energy, influence, and enlightenment. The Bible makes it clear that the Holy Spirit is a divine person who moves on believers to accomplish God's purposes on earth. That is a critical distinction to understand, as evangelist R. A. Torrey explained: "If we think of the Holy Spirit only as an impersonal power or influence, then our thought will constantly be, 'How can I get hold of and use the Holy Spirit?'; but if we think of Him in the biblical way as a divine Person, infinitely wise, infinitely holy, infinitely tender, then our thought will constantly be, 'How can the Holy Spirit get hold of and use me?'"

The Holy Spirit is not just an illumination or inspiration that comes to our minds so we can see truth. He is a person who himself knows the things of God and reveals them to us.
—Fuchsia Pickett

Those who demote the Holy Spirit to the role of an impersonal force either reject or fail to understand the biblical description of who the Spirit is and what the Spirit does. The Bible presents the Holy Spirit as a person. Jesus consistently used a personal pronoun (such as *he*) and not an impersonal pronoun (*it*) when referring to the Holy Spirit. Passages in the New Testament show that the Holy Spirit

The Holy Spirit came down on him in the form of a dove. Then a voice came from heaven, saying, "You are my Son, whom I love, and I am very pleased with you."

Luke 3:22 NCV

- speaks to believers, as to Philip (Acts 8:29), the believers at Antioch (Acts 13:1–4), and Peter (Acts 10:19–20);

- intercedes in prayer on behalf of Christians (Romans 8:26) just as Jesus Christ does (Romans 8:34);

- testifies to the truth of who Jesus is (John 15:26–27);

- teaches believers (John 14:26);

- prevents Christians from acting in conflict with God's will (Acts 16:6–7).

The Holy Spirit empowers believers in a multitude of ways, just as the Spirit empowered Jesus during his earthly ministry (Luke 4:14–21; Matthew 12:28). The Spirit equips you to do God's work on earth by strengthening you and giving you the spiritual gifts, such as evangelism and teaching, needed for the task at hand. The Spirit prompts you to do things that please God and avoid the rest. Remember the last time you were tempted to stretch the truth, but suddenly the words just wouldn't come out? That was the Spirit loving you enough to stop you from saying something you'd regret later.

Do not let the Spirit remain a mystery to you. Get to know who the Spirit is and how the Spirit works in your life. Armed with that understanding, you will no longer question how the Spirit acts in your life.

what's essential

Getting to know the Spirit is as essential as getting to know God, because the Spirit is God. Your spiritual life will change dramatically once you realize how important it is to access the Spirit's gifts, guidance, and power in your everyday life.

DO get to know the Holy Spirit and how the Spirit works in your life.

DO learn to rely on the Spirit whenever God calls you to accomplish a particular task for him.

DON'T think of the Holy Spirit as an impersonal force; the Spirit is personal and actively involved in your life.

DON'T try to figure out how you can use the Holy Spirit; ask instead how the Spirit can use you.

What Do I Believe?

Forgiveness

Oh, what joy for those whose disobedience is forgiven, whose sin is put out of sight! Yes, what joy for those whose record the LORD has cleared of guilt, whose lives are lived in complete honesty!

Psalm 32:1–2 NLT

Forgiveness does not change the past, but it does enlarge the future.

Paul Boese

"I can forgive but I cannot forget" is only another way of saying "I will not forgive." Forgiveness ought to be like a canceled note—torn in two, and burned up, so that it never can be shown against one.

Henry Ward Beecher

Believe What the Bible Says

The Bible has long been under attack, but never more so than in recent years. Some charge that it is an antiquated, politically incorrect book written not by God but by mortal men with questionable motives. Is the Bible inspired or not? How you answer that question profoundly affects your walk with God.

All Scripture is given by inspiration of God, and is profitable for doctrine, for reproof, for correction, for instruction in righteousness.

2 Timothy 3:16 NKJV

Perhaps you have heard the recent arguments against the trustworthiness and therefore the authority of the Bible. In some cases, critics conclude that while the Bible stands apart as a religious and literary masterpiece, its content has little relevance to contemporary life. In other cases, cynics ascribe sinister intentions to the early Christian leaders who decided which sixty-six books would be included in the Bible. Pop culture even weighs in, with Dan Brown's *The Da Vinci Code* leading the way in raising questions about the Scriptures.

The fact that questions are being asked is not the problem. But an unquestioned denial of the truth of the Bible is no better than an unquestioned allegiance to it; distrusting the Bible just because Dan Brown cast doubts on it isn't all that

A loving Personality dominates the Bible, walking among the trees of the garden and breathing fragrance over every scene. Always a living Person is present, speaking, pleading, loving, working, and manifesting himself.

A. W. Tozer

different from believing the Bible just because your pastor has faith in it.

So go ahead—ask the critical questions whose answers will settle the debate for you once and for all. The Bible can certainly bear your scrutiny. And by examining the issues for yourself, you will have the confidence of knowing that you came by your beliefs about the Bible honestly.

 One of these days some simple soul will pick up the Book of God, read it, and believe it. Then the rest of us will be embarrassed.
—Leonard Ravenhill

Here are some of the questions you will want to ask, along with references for the verses that Christians use to support their belief in the authority of the Bible:

- Is the Bible truly the inspired Word of God? (2 Timothy 3:16)

- But weren't the words written down by imperfect men? (2 Peter 1:20–21)

- What about the claims that the Bible is "inerrant"—free of error? (Matthew 5:18; John 10:35)

- Of what use is the Bible to me, living in the twenty-first century? (Hebrews 4:12)

Why, though, is answering these questions so important? Many will say that it is important because denying the Bible's authority places people on a slippery slope toward denying the essential teachings of the Christian faith. But the answer is actually much larger—and much smaller—than that. The Bible represents who God is and depicts God's involvement with humanity. It also offers guidance to individuals—to you personally. Your answers to the questions above will affect your view of God as well as your relationship with him.

Theologian J. I. Packer believes support for the inerrancy of Scripture also serves to protect Christians from disregarding important biblical teachings, ignoring instructions regarding worship and service, and resolving knotty scriptural problems by denying that the Bible is the inspired Word of God. "It is because the word 'inerrant' makes these methodological points about handling the Bible, ruling out in advance the use of mental procedures that can only lead to reduced and distorted versions of Christianity, that it is so valuable and, I think, so much valued by those who embrace it," Packer wrote.

In your investigation of the Bible, remember one more biblical concept: the Bible is a means to an end, not an end in itself. It is a means toward recognizing the One you should worship and not an object of worship of its own. "We do not believe in Christ because He is in the Bible," wrote author Claxton Monro. "We believe in the Bible because Christ is in us." That is a significant distinction to keep in mind and a guiding

interesting to note

Familiarity with the Bible was long considered the mark of an educated person. A dramatic shift in that perception prompted C. S. Lewis to predict that the Bible would soon be read "almost exclusively by Christians." To make sure that doesn't happen, BiblicalLiteracy.org promotes biblical literacy in high schools and colleges.

The word of God is living and active. Sharper than any double-edged sword, it penetrates even to dividing soul and spirit, joints and marrow; it judges the thoughts and attitudes of the heart.

Hebrews 4:12 NIV

principle for you to follow as you determine what you believe about the Bible.

And as you grapple with your questions, keep reading the Bible. The Bible itself may prove to be the only answer you need as you witness its truths unfolding in your life. Many Christians have come to believe in its authority in just that way.

what's essential

In its entirety, the Bible is God's message to his people. Whether you accept that message and live your life in accordance with the Bible is entirely up to you. Just make sure that your decision to accept or reject is a result of honest inquiry rather than personal opinion.

DO trust the Holy Spirit to guide you into the whole truth about the Bible and the claims regarding its inspiration and inerrancy.

DO continue to read the Bible even if you are unsure about it; it contains many of the answers to your questions.

DON'T forget that the sole object of your worship is God alone and not the Bible, as important as it is.

DON'T blindly accept cultural opinions about the Bible; discover the truth for yourself.

Understand Christianity's Claims

In the early centuries of Christianity, the greatest threat was intense, deadly persecution. But the faith of early believers was so strong that the faith grew. Among the greatest threats to the twenty-first-century church is a chipping away at the distinctive beliefs of the faith. Is your faith strong enough to meet this challenge?

From its inception, Christianity was set apart from all other religions as a distinctive expression of faith. This was no religion whose rules and regulations and rituals were designed to appease an angry god—or gods. Neither was it a religion that required its adherents to work their way to a blissful afterlife through a rigid course of self-denial, self-humiliation, and even self-flagellation. No, Christianity was, is, and always will be a relationship with God through his Son, Jesus Christ, by the power of the Holy Spirit.

At least, that is Christianity in its purest form.

For more than two millennia, human beings—some of them well-meaning Christians—have tampered with that ideal and tried to reduce

This is what I told you while I was still with you: everything which is written concerning Me in the Law of Moses and the Prophets and the Psalms must be fulfilled.

Luke 24:44 AMP

Christianity is just Christ—nothing more and nothing less. It is a way of life, and He is that way. It is the truth about human destiny, and He is that truth.

R. J. Campbell

Christianity to a rules-and-regulations religion. But so far, the pure form of the faith has always managed to prevail and overcome human interference.

Today, though, things have changed. Global communications have brought other faiths into American homes and communities that were once predominantly Christian, whether in practice or in name only—and much of what people heard was attractive, reasonable, and inspirational. Nonbiblical ideas became incorporated into Christian thought. That is a simplified description of a complex, multifaceted process that has begun to erode the Christian faith, but one undeniable result has been a confused Christian community.

 The greatest proof of Christianity for others is not how far a man can logically analyze his reasons for believing, but how far in practice he will stake his life on his belief.
—T. S. Eliot

When you factor in tolerance and political correctness, you add fear to that confusion. Many Christians are afraid to defend the very concepts that are foundational to true Christianity out of fear that they may offend someone and come across as intolerant; defending the faith without appearing to be unloving and arrogant is in fact an uphill battle for contemporary Christians.

Nineteenth-century monk John Neville Figgis believed the resulting division is inevitable: "[Christianity] drives a wedge between its own adherents and the disciples of every other philosophy or religion, however lofty or soaring. And they will not see this; they will tell you that really your views and theirs are the same thing, and only differ in words, which, if only you were a little more highly trained, you would understand . . . Many [Christians] think a little good-will is all that is needed to bridge the gulf—a little amiability and mutual explanation, a more careful use of phrases, would soon accommodate Christianity to fashionable modes of speaking and thinking, and destroy all causes of provocation. So they would. But they would destroy also its one inalienable attraction: that of being . . . a wonder, and a beauty, and a terror."

To fully embrace Christianity is to reject the basis of other faiths. As with the question of the divinity of Christ, there really is no middle ground here; Christ is either the Son of God or a fraud, and Christianity is either a unique expression of faith based on a relationship or just one of many other religions, utterly without distinction.

Do you believe that? What do you believe about the claims of Christianity? If you consider Christianity to be one of many paths to God, what do you make of the claim that Jesus is the only way to the Father? These are important questions that you need to ask yourself and answer for yourself. These questions are a continuation of those that have come

interesting to note

While the number of nondenominational Protestants has seen some growth in recent years, a 2008 study from the Pew Forum on Religion and Public Life revealed that another group showed the greatest gain in numbers. That group was the "religiously unaffiliated"—those who no longer identify with any organized religion.

We did not follow cleverly invented stories when we told you about the power and coming of our Lord Jesus Christ, but we were eyewitnesses of his majesty.

2 Peter 1:16 NIV

before; if you believe Jesus is who he says he is, if you believe in the biblical account of the bodily resurrection of Jesus Christ, if you believe that the Bible is the Word of God, then it follows that you believe Christianity's claims—the very nature and foundation of the Christian faith make it difficult for you to say you believe otherwise.

what's essential

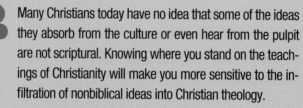 Many Christians today have no idea that some of the ideas they absorb from the culture or even hear from the pulpit are not scriptural. Knowing where you stand on the teachings of Christianity will make you more sensitive to the infiltration of nonbiblical ideas into Christian theology.

DO study the specific characteristics of Christianity to determine its uniqueness when compared to other faiths.

DO be aware that the acceptance of unbiblical ideas from other religions can weaken Christian theology.

DON'T be afraid to examine the teachings of other faiths through the lens of Christianity.

DON'T allow fear and confusion to prevent you from fully embracing the teachings of Christianity.

Clarify What Faith Is

To the Christian, faith is a way of life. Far more than being convinced that a certain set of beliefs is true, faith is a deep and abiding confidence in an unseen reality. Others may say that seeing is believing, but the Christian says believing is not seeing. And that bewilders those who do not believe.

The fundamental fact of existence is that this trust in God, this faith, is the firm foundation under everything that makes life worth living. It's our handle on what we can't see.

Hebrews 11:1 MSG

How do you define *faith*? Better yet, how would you describe your own faith? If you are a Christian, your faith likely involves a conviction that God is real, that his Son, Jesus Christ, is the promised Savior, that the Bible is the authoritative Word of God, and so forth. But faith is not a stagnant belief system; it is a dynamic perspective on life that grows as you mature in your relationship with God.

Hebrews 11:1 defines *faith* as "the assurance of things hoped for, the conviction of things not seen" (NASB)—and that carries with it the element of trust. To have faith that something you hope for will come to pass or that something you cannot see is real, you need to trust that someone, or something, is in control of those things you need faith for.

Faith is a response on our part, the obedient response of our wills to who God is and what He says.

John White

As a Christian, you know that someone is God. And because of your faith in him, you can trust him to be at the controls of your life—and life in general. "As Christians we accept one foundational truth—God—and everything else makes sense," John MacArthur once wrote. "An atheist denies God and has to accept incredible explanations for everything else. It takes more faith to deny God than to believe in Him."

 At the beginning of every act of faith, there is often a seed of fear. For great acts of faith are seldom born out of calm calculation.
—Max Lucado

But faith needs to be exercised in order to remain alive and grow stronger. If you've been a Christian for a while, you should have a deeper faith in God than you did at the start. Think about how your faith has grown over the years. God uses whatever he wants to cause a person's faith to grow, but most often what he uses fits into four areas:

- *The Bible.* Romans 10:17 says "Faith comes from hearing, and hearing by the word of Christ" (NASB). For a largely illiterate society, *hearing* was the operative word. For you, reading the word is also a pathway to a stronger faith. In both his gospel and one of his epistles, John emphasizes that he wrote what he did so others would come to faith in Christ.

- *Fellowship with other Christians.* Hebrews 3:12–14 and other passages in the New Testament urge Christians to encourage

one another so their faith will be strength-
ened.

- *Obedience to God.* By obeying God, Christians
  will come to have greater faith in Jesus and
  all that he taught (John 7:17).

- *God's activity in your life.* Whenever you experience answered prayer or any other evidence
  of God's personal involvement in your life,
  your faith grows.

Look at that list again. For every point, there is a
counterpoint at work that can destroy your faith.
If you ignore the Bible, over time you may forget
all God has promised you and all the evidence
he has offered of his love and compassion for
you. If you avoid worshiping with other Christians (Hebrews 10:25) or cultivating Christian
friendships, you will have no one to encourage
you in your faith. If you regularly disobey God,
well, you will prove to yourself that you really do
not have faith in him. And if you disregard those
times that God breaks through your indifference
and blesses you in ways you do not deserve, your
faith, such as it is, will likely wither and die.

Faith is what enables you to have victory
in your life, because faith sees beyond the

interesting to note

Faith can be incremental.
It is not as if you either
have faith or you don't;
you can have little faith
(Matthew 6:30), strong
or weak faith (Romans
4:19–20), great faith
(Matthew 8:10), growing
faith (2 Thessalonians
1:3), all faith (1 Corinthians 13:2), or be full of
faith (Acts 6:5).

Every God-begotten
person conquers the
world's ways. The
conquering power that
brings the world to its
knees is our faith.

1 John 5:4 MSG

challenges of everyday living and points you to a world beyond, a dimension where "things hoped for" find their substance and an unseen reality waits to reveal all truth to you.

what's essential

Without faith, it is impossible to please God (Hebrews 11:6). The desire to please God should be an essential component of your relationship with him. Whenever you exercise your faith, you show God you believe that "He is, and that He is a rewarder of those who diligently seek Him" (11:6 NKJV).

DO read the Bible on a regular basis to strengthen your faith and cause it to grow.

DO understand that your faith will grow stronger with time, knowledge, and experience in obeying God.

DON'T ignore God's work in your life; keep a journal of answered prayer to remind you of all he has done for you.

DON'T avoid being around Christians when you feel your faith falter; that is when you need their company the most.

Catch a Glimpse of Eternity

After a semi struck Don Piper's car head-on, Piper was pronounced dead. Before he was revived, he says he spent 90 Minutes in Heaven—the title of the best seller based on his experience. In a culture both fascinated by and fearful of the afterlife, it is no wonder Piper's book sold half a million copies.

God made a promise to us, and we are waiting for a new heaven and a new earth where goodness lives.

2 Peter 3:13–14 NCV

It is understandable that so many readers are drawn to books about personal visits to heaven. For those outside the Christian faith, the accounts help to assuage some of their fears, especially if the writer describes heaven as a place that welcomes everyone. For Christians, many of the accounts confirm the biblical record about what heaven is like. All the books, of course, provoke controversy; did the Christian writers really visit heaven, or did they simply dream about what they expected to see? No one knows but God.

Thankfully, you can get a glimpse of what heaven is like without having to die, because the Bible records the apostle John's vision of heaven in Revelation 21:11: "It shone with the glory of God, and its brilliance was like that of a very precious jewel,

We talk about heaven being so far away. It is within speaking distance to those who belong there. Heaven is a prepared place for a prepared people.

Dwight L. Moody

like a jasper, clear as crystal" (NIV). John went on to describe the New Jerusalem in great detail and even provided its dimensions. In verse 18, he picked up the visual description once again: "The wall was made of jasper, and the city of pure gold, as pure as glass" (NIV), and the foundation of the city was decorated with precious stones, including sapphire, emerald, topaz, and amethyst.

 If you have not chosen the Kingdom of God first, it will in the end make no difference what you have chosen instead.
—William Law

That is just a small portion of the physical description of heaven. In addition to the mansion Jesus has prepared for you (John 14:2), there are more treasures, such as

- hope laid up for you in heaven (Colossians 1:5);

- hope and an inheritance (1 Peter 1:3–4);

- better and enduring possessions (Hebrews 10:34);

- a place where there will be no more death, mourning, crying, or pain (Revelation 21:4);

- healing (Revelation 22:2);

- a place where Christians will serve and reign (Revelation 22:3–5);

- a heavenly kingdom (2 Timothy 4:18);

- an eternal kingdom (2 Peter 1:11);

- a place of righteousness (2 Peter 3:13).

As wonderful as all that sounds, it barely scratches the surface of what is to come. Throughout eternity, God's glory will provide the only light you will ever need. Your body will be transformed, and whatever suffering your body has had to endure on earth will be eradicated in heaven. You will join with a choir of angels in bowing before God, rejoicing, and singing praises to him.

Revelation 21:3 describes the best heavenly aspect of all: total, unbroken fellowship with God. "For the Christian, heaven is where Jesus is," theologian William Barclay wrote. "We do not need to speculate on what heaven will be like. It is enough to know that we will be forever with Him."

How does all this line up with your anticipation of heaven? If you have settled the issue of where you will spend eternity, you are no doubt looking forward to that time of unbroken fellowship with Jesus. If you have not, it is time to settle the not-so-small matter of where you will spend eternity. Your life on earth is simply a brief moment compared to eternity; your greatest hope in this life is not only that you can have fellowship with Jesus in the here and now but more so that you will be able to experience eternal life in his presence.

As C. S. Lewis observed, "There are better things ahead than any we leave behind." Without the

interesting to note

The Old Testament records several visions of God in heaven "seated on a throne, high and exalted, and the train of his robe filled the temple" (Isaiah 6:1 NIV) and "sitting on His throne, and all the host of heaven standing by, on His right hand and on His left" (1 Kings 22:19 NKJV).

I consider that the sufferings of this present time are not worthy to be compared with the glory that is to be revealed to us.
Romans 8:18 NASB

hope of heaven—the hope of being in God's presence forever—life after death would be no life at all. Better things await you, including "a building from God, an eternal house in heaven, not built by human hands" (2 Corinthians 5:1 NIV)—and for much longer than ninety minutes.

what's essential

Once you are assured that heaven will be your future home, focus your attention on sharing God with others here on earth. Heaven will be full of surprises, and there is a lot to look forward to. You can count on that.

DO understand that what you know about heaven now is but a shadow of what your eternal dwelling place will really be like.

DO settle the question of where you will spend eternity.

DON'T forget that your time on earth is a mere moment compared to eternity.

DON'T serve God just because of the hope of heaven; serve God because he is worthy of it.

Spread the Good News

What comes to mind when you hear the word evangelism? Duty? Obligation? Fear? How about love? When you begin to see evangelism as an act of love, showing others the way to God becomes a joy and a privilege. And it is easier than you may think.

People come to Christ in many ways. A sermon, a book, a movie, even a song can drive a person straight into the arms of God. But most often, the influence of an individual Christian turns a person in Christ's direction.

That influence can take many forms. You do not have to be a great communicator to be influential; if that was the case, few Christians would dare to spread the good news. You only have to convey to others the love of Christ, how that love changed your life, and how that love can change the life of the person with whom you are sharing.

How you do that depends on you. Answer this question: if you did not know Christ, how would you prefer that someone share Christ with you?

> My message and my preaching were very plain. Rather than using clever and persuasive speeches, I relied only on the power of the Holy Spirit. I did this so you would trust not in human wisdom but in the power of God.
>
> **1 Corinthians 2:4–5 NLT**

> We will win the world when we realize that fellowship, not evangelism, must be our primary emphasis. When we demonstrate the Big Miracle of Love, it won't be necessary for us to go out—they will come in.
>
> **Jess Moody**

Your answer most likely reflects the method of evangelism that is most suitable for you to use. See which of the methods below works best for you and give it a try. Or mix it up a bit, and give them all a try.

- *Friendship.* Theologian J. I. Packer said this: "The right to talk intimately to another person about the Lord Jesus Christ has to be earned, and you earn it by convincing him that you are his friend, and really care about him . . . If you wish to do personal evangelism, then you ought to pray for the gift of friendship." But it must be an authentic friendship that will survive even if the person rejects Christ. And it takes time, because building a friendship takes time. Jesus befriended religious society's outcasts, such as prostitutes, and he took some heat for it. You may too.

 Evangelism is the deepest and most profound social action in the world, because it deals with the root of the problem, not with the symptoms.
—Luis Palau

- *Lifestyle.* This is evangelism by example. The idea is that if you can demonstrate Christianity in action through godly living, kindness, compassion, and good works, people will be drawn to you because they see Christ in you, whether they realize it or not. That gives you an opportunity to explain why you live the way you do, sharing Christ with them in the process.

- *One-on-one.* Similar to friendship and lifestyle evangelism, one-on-one evangelism is distinguished from those methods by being more intentional. Instead of waiting for a friendship to grow or for your lifestyle to have a positive effect, a one-on-one evangelist is more apt to share the gospel with strangers who demonstrate a specific need or an openness to the gospel. An example would be if you saw someone crying in a public place—say, in a coffee shop or on a park bench—and felt led to comfort the person and share Christ at the same time.

- *Online.* The possibilities here are endless; you could start a blog or create a Web site on any number of topics that would pique the interest of someone in need of Christ. To make this truly evangelistic, however, you need to make sure there are opportunities for interaction and comments. By responding to comments made by visitors to the site, Christians who are shy by nature can have a dramatic impact on others.

- *The arts.* If you are a creative person, this may be the approach to take. Use your talent for literary, visual, or performing arts as a vehicle to present the gospel to others. To make it more personal, be prepared to share Christ with those who come to your launch parties, book signings, art show openings, or musical

Go then and make disciples of all the nations, baptizing them into the name of the Father and of the Son and of the Holy Spirit.

Matthew 28:19 AMP

performances, using your artwork as a springboard for opening the conversation.

Ask God to show you how you can best share the gospel with others. You may discover a whole new form of evangelism.

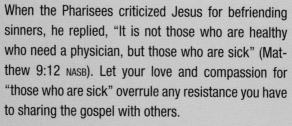

what's essential

 When the Pharisees criticized Jesus for befriending sinners, he replied, "It is not those who are healthy who need a physician, but those who are sick" (Matthew 9:12 NASB). Let your love and compassion for "those who are sick" overrule any resistance you have to sharing the gospel with others.

DO show that you care about the person you are sharing Christ with; let love set the tone for your relationship.

DO ask God to show you new and creative ways of spreading the good news of Christ to others.

DON'T force it; people can sense when others are pushing an agenda on them, and it is especially distasteful when the agenda is evangelistic.

DON'T forget to pray before you open up about Christ, while you are sharing the gospel, and after you are finished.

What Do I Believe?

JUBILATION

This is GOD'S work. We rub our eyes—we can hardly believe it! This is the very day GOD acted—let's celebrate and be festive! Salvation now, GOD. Salvation now! Oh yes, GOD—a free and full life!

Psalm 118:23–25 MSG

A tongue filled with laughter and praise is a reflection of a heart filled to overflowing with the joy of the Lord.

Mike Hoskins

Seek to cultivate a buoyant, joyous sense of the crowded kindnesses of God in your daily life.

Alexander MacLaren

Develop a Biblical Worldview

Like clockwork, conversations on the topic of a biblical worldview rev up every four years as presidential candidates take to the campaign trail. But this is a conversation much too important to ignore the rest of the time—and that is because your worldview affects a lot of what you say and do.

Be sure that no one leads you away with false and empty teaching that is only human, which comes from the ruling spirits of this world, and not from Christ.

Colossians 2:8 NCV

Without God, man is the chance product of unthinking fate, and so of little worth. The current loss of identity and the emergence of the faceless man in today's culture are testimony to the effects of losing our God. The knowledge of God is given in the same movement in which we know ourselves.

Clark H. Pinnock

A political candidate's worldview, whether it is described using that term or not, has become a litmus test for many voters. Presumably, if you know a candidate's worldview—essentially, the basis for the person's philosophy of life—you can predict with some degree of accuracy the way he or she will vote or guide the country on specific issues. That is important, but politicians are not the only people whose worldviews are crucial.

Your worldview is equally important, if not more so. You make decisions every day that affect the people around you—your friends, neighbors, co-workers or employees, spouse, children, even the strangers you encounter on the street. A worldview based on the belief that a loving God interacts with humanity is vastly different from worldviews based on the belief that God is an impersonal cosmic force or an angry judge out to get everyone. Likewise, adherents of those three worldviews will treat others in vastly different ways.

But what exactly is a biblical worldview? A basic list of the essentials of a biblical worldview would likely include the following:

- God, the Creator of the universe, is all-knowing, all-powerful, and always present.

- People were created in the image of God but need to be reconciled to him.

- Jesus, who was fully God and fully man while on earth, lived a sinless life and sacrificed his life to save people from their sins.

- The Bible is the authoritative Word of God and can be trusted to offer guidance and correction.

 He who marries the spirit of the age soon becomes a widower.
—Dean Inge

That's a good starting point, and it is especially helpful to keep the list short on surveys. But because a worldview is highly personal, you are likely to find Christians who would add any number of beliefs to that list, including these:

- God wants to redeem the earth as well as humankind.

- God is male and female, personal and transcendent, and has characteristics that are known and unknown.

- The world's brokenness is a result of humanity's sin.

- Every life has value.

You may have more suggestions about which beliefs are critical to developing a biblical worldview. One characteristic of a personal worldview is that it is not set in stone. As God gives you insight and as you read about different worldviews, you can add more beliefs that you feel are essential.

Now that you know what a worldview is, it is time to examine why it is so important to develop a biblical worldview. In the first place, defining your worldview helps you clarify what you really believe and what you consider to be of greatest importance among those beliefs. You may believe, for example, that singing the Scriptures is a great way to praise God, but that belief may not be fundamental to your worldview—your philosophy of life.

Whether you are aware of it or not, your worldview shapes your actions and your thinking. If you believe Jesus is the Lord of your life and you are committed to living in line with his will, your decisions will reflect that even when you are not conscious of it. Your refusal to support a company that takes advantage of the poor may not be something you have grappled with theologically, for instance, but it reflects Jesus' concern for the underprivileged.

Having the mind of Christ (1 Corinthians 2:16), in fact, is the best starting point for developing a biblical worldview; every other aspect of your belief system will fall in line under the headship of Christ. When you get to know Jesus intimately, you cannot help but see the world through a biblical lens. When Jesus' worldview becomes your worldview, everything you do and say is a reflection of the mind of Christ.

what's essential

Your worldview helps you make sense of the world. Life can be confusing and full of complications and contradictions. By intentionally developing a biblical worldview, you bring the mind of Christ to bear on every situation, every challenge, and every temptation you face in life.

DO take some time to define and develop your own worldview.

DO be aware that your belief system and philosophy of life factors in to every decision you make, whether or not you are conscious of it.

DON'T compromise on what you believe, because your beliefs create the lens through which you see the world and interact with it.

DON'T consider your worldview to be set in stone; make allowances for further insights from God about what is critical to your belief system.

Commit Your Life to Jesus

This essential may seem like a no-brainer. Of course you need to commit your life to God. You probably did that years ago; but maybe you need to evaluate that commitment. The world has changed, you've changed, your relationship with God has changed, and maybe it is time for a refresher.

Committing your life to God means resolving to obey him and giving him control over everything. It is not uncommon for Christians to profess faith in God but fail to take the all-important second step of moving aside and giving him control. Sometimes, they are not even aware that a second step is necessary.

As William Barclay put it, "A conversion is incomplete if it does not leave Jesus Christ in the central place in one's life." Maybe your conversion was complete at one time, and you did give God central place in your life. But you know how life can be. Time goes by, obligations increase, your schedule gets crowded with lots of other things, and little by little, Jesus gets nudged off to the side. He no longer has the central place. He is no longer in control of everything. Without even realizing it, you have regained control of it all.

Consider the way Paul described the Christian life in Acts 17:28: "In Him we live and move and exist" (NASB). Does that sound like a description of your daily life? Do you live and move and exist in God? If not, there is a great likelihood that a recommitment is in order.

Each of us is an innkeeper who decides if there is room for Jesus.
—Neal A. Maxwell

The only thing that complicates a commitment, or a recommitment, is your heart's attitude. It is easy enough to verbally commit your life to God, but your heart is another matter. Think through what it means to turn over control of your daily life: your schedule, work, habits, marriage, family, friendships, entertainment, outside activities, hobbies—and every last one of your possessions. That is a tall order. Are you up to it?

But look at the benefits. You will have the opportunity to

- jump-start your spiritual growth;

- experience a renewed relationship with God;

- explore a vision for ministry you have allowed to die;

- rediscover your spiritual purpose;

- become transformed into the likeness of Christ;

- restore relationships that need restoring;

- become free of attachments to things that may not be good for you or the best for you;

- let go of bad habits and replace them with good ones;

- reduce the number of regrets you will have later in life;

- live the abundant life God promised to his followers.

Is it worth it? Of course it is. Is it still a scary proposition? Well, yes, if you find your security in maintaining control over your own life and you fear the loss of that security in turning control over to God. "The beautiful thing about this adventure called faith," wrote Chuck Swindoll, "is that we can count on Him never to lead us astray." Giving God control over your life offers you greater security than your own control ever will.

Look at what Romans 12:1–2 has to say about your situation: "Here's what I want you to do, God helping you: Take your everyday, ordinary life—your sleeping, eating, going-to-work, and walking-around life—and place it before God as an offering. Embracing what God does for you is the best thing you can do for him. Don't become so well-adjusted to your culture that you fit into it without even thinking. Instead, fix your attention on God. You'll be changed from the inside out.

Readily recognize what he wants from you, and quickly respond to it. Unlike the culture around you, always dragging you down to its level of immaturity, God brings the best out of you, develops well-formed maturity in you" (MSG).

It is time—time to give God control of your life once again.

what's essential

Committing your life to God involves confessing your sin (1 John 1:9), giving yourself completely over to him (Romans 12:1), and yielding control to him on a daily basis (Romans 6:11–14). It also involves turning back to him when you sense you are trying to regain the control.

DO be honest with yourself about where God stands in your life; is he center stage or in the wings?

DO recognize that the security you feel in controlling your own life is a false security.

DON'T be afraid to turn control over to God. He has always known what is best for you and always will.

DON'T neglect confession; you can have the assurance of knowing that God stands ready to forgive.

Study the Bible

It is a rare Christian who hasn't studied the Bible in some way. Many churches host group Bible studies. Scripture study materials line bookstore shelves. The Internet offers an abundance of study opportunities—some good, some not so good. But Christians used another Bible study method for millennia, and it is staging a bit of a comeback.

Until the twentieth century, Christians studied the Bible using commentaries and other reference works written by scholars and religious leaders. Those authors had made it their life's work to research biblical passages in the original languages, for example, in order to illuminate the Scriptures for laypeople. It wasn't unusual for a lay Christian to dedicate Sunday afternoons to an intense study of the Bible, reading a passage of Scripture and any related verses, and then turning to commentaries that would shed light on the meaning of the passage.

Some people still do this, but their numbers are dwindling. Surveys conducted by both professional pollsters and individual churches reveal that intense Bible study is yet another victim of the busyness of American life. Some date the demise of Bible study to the widespread repeal of blue laws, which among other things prohibited stores from opening on Sundays and which paved the way for longer shopping hours overall. That meant more distractions for the public and longer and later hours for store owners and employees.

Churches, religious organizations, and groups of individuals attempt to fill the void by offering group Bible study meetings. These are helpful, but they add another activity outside the home to an already crowded schedule—and are not meant to be a substitute for your own study of the Bible.

No one ever graduates from Bible study until he meets its Author face to face.
—Everett Harris

But how on earth do you get started with a personal study of the Bible? The irony is that although that seems challenging, it has never been easier. Virtually every commentary that is in the public domain—that is, for which the copyright has expired—is available online, as are online Bibles that provide links to a wealth of study materials. Bookstores offer the latest scholarly research in recently published reference works, as well as Bible study guides designed for busy people. In addition, Bible studies now cater to the special interests and needs of nearly every demographic—men, women, youth, and children, of course; but also couples, singles, parents, college students, soldiers, and so forth.

Study and be eager and do your utmost to present yourself to God approved (tested by trial), a workman who has no cause to be ashamed, correctly analyzing and accurately dividing [rightly handling and skillfully teaching] the Word of Truth.

2 Timothy 2:15 AMP

No matter what kind of guide you use, there are many ways to study the Bible—by topic, book, biblical character, chronology, concept, and so forth. Here's one way you can get started; you will eventually find the method that is best for you.

- Pray. Ask the Holy Spirit to lead you to a passage to study and to reveal the truth of those verses to you.

- Read the section carefully and see what pops out at you. Maybe it will be a word, a phrase, or a concept, like *atonement*—the forgiveness of sin through death. That could lead you to a deeper understanding of what the word means (using a lexicon or other language-oriented reference book) or a topical study of how the Israelites viewed atonement and how that compares with the Christian understanding of the concept.

- Read any cross-references—other Bible verses that are related to the primary passage you are studying. These are often found in the margins of a printed Bible or in links of an online Bible.

- Ask the Spirit to clarify anything you do not understand, either by directing you to other sources or by simply revealing it to you directly.

The most important step is applying what you've learned to your everyday life. The Holy Spirit doesn't lead people to study the Bible just so they can walk away with a head full of knowledge. The application of a study on, say, atonement may not be obvious, but it may result in a deeper gratitude for Jesus' work on the cross. And that will affect your relationship with him from that point forward.

what's essential

Bible study can become addictive. You can lose yourself in the depths of the Bible and come away feeling as if you've just scratched the surface. You may even discover that you cannot wait to get back to the Bible—at a time when you hadn't even planned to study.

DO set aside an appointed time to devote to personal Bible study, in addition to your regular Bible reading.

DO expect the Holy Spirit to guide you, educate you, and train you as you study the Bible.

DON'T study the Bible simply to acquire an impressive amount of knowledge.

DON'T use what you've learned in an inappropriate way—like starting a biblical argument because you think you are armed with winning ammunition.

Meditate on Scripture

Meditation, in some form, is practiced by people of all faiths—and people of no faith. A person can meditate on words, images, concepts, sounds, ideas, and so forth, whether spiritual or secular, godly or ungodly. But Christian meditation is in a class by itself. Ultimately, God is its focus.

For a variety of reasons, meditation is not mentioned as frequently in Christian churches as are other spiritual practices. The practice fell into disfavor decades ago as Eastern religions began to permeate Western culture and the Eastern form of meditation became popular. The practice has yet to recover from the hit it took when Christian leaders warned about the dangers of unbiblical meditation.

But there is a type of meditation that is decidedly scriptural—and the Scriptures even tell Christians to practice it. This kind of meditation always points the one who practices it toward God, whether the person is meditating on a verse of Scripture or a piece of music. If it meets the test of Scripture—if it is true, noble, just, pure, lovely, reputable, virtuous, and praiseworthy (Philippians 4:8)—it is worthy of meditation.

Some traditions tend to complicate the act of meditation with instructions on how to sit and how to breathe and so forth, and settling in to a comfortable but not sleep-inducing position is certainly useful. But meditation is a simple practice that involves deep reflection on one thing and one thing only. If you choose to meditate on a portion of Scripture, for example, you keep your mind and your heart focused on those verses, asking the Holy Spirit to reveal their meaning to you. If your mind wanders, and it most likely will, deal with the distraction or dismiss it, but return to the meditation. You may or may not receive new insights—sometimes, they occur to you weeks later—but you've spent time in the presence of the Lord, and that is always time well spent.

 One cannot begin to face the real difficulties of a life of prayer and meditation unless one is first perfectly content to be a beginner. —Thomas Merton

The people you meet in the pages of Scripture would agree. Examples of meditation and references to the practice are found throughout the Bible. In the Old Testament, Isaac's first glimpse of Rebekah, the love of his life, came as he was meditating in a field at dusk (Genesis 24:63–67); as a young shepherd boy, David meditated on God throughout the night watches and became wiser than his teachers as a result (Psalm 119:99). God commanded Joshua to meditate on his law "day and night" (Joshua 1:8 NKJV), while that practice is echoed in Psalm 1, where one who meditates day and night is described as blessed. In the New Testament, Paul told Timothy to meditate on the spiritual gifts

interesting to note

The Israelites took literally the command to not let the law "depart from your mouth"(Joshua 1:8 NKJV); throughout the day they whispered their meditation, quietly speaking the words out of obedience and the conviction that hearing Scripture in their own voice would help them recall it. Some Christians continue that practice today.

Tremble, and do not sin; meditate in your heart upon your bed, and be still. Selah.

Psalm 4:4 NASB

and the ministry God had given him (1 Timothy 4:15).

Clearly, meditation is among the spiritual practices God expects his people to follow. But why? What is the point of meditation? Why does God want you to meditate? Christian meditation accomplishes the following:

- You draw closer to God as you contemplate who he is and all that he has done (Psalms 77:12; 119:148).

- You become transformed—more like Christ—as your mind is renewed by dwelling on "things above" (Colossians 3:1–2 NKJV).

- As you meditate on the Bible, its richness and truths seep into your spirit and become a part of you (Psalm 119:167).

- You will have spiritual success (Joshua 1:8).

- You will likely get in the habit of dwelling on those things that are acceptable to God (Philippians 4:8).

Regardless of what you are meditating on, slow down and devote an adequate amount of time to the practice. There is no magic formula for how long that should be; meditating on Scripture or another devotional writing may or may not require more time than meditating on an inspirational painting. With practice, you will become more aware of the point at which your time of meditation has run its course.

what's essential

If you want to draw closer to God, you have to spend time with him. Setting aside a certain amount of time on a regular basis to focus exclusively on him—that's a guaranteed way to get to know him better and develop an intimate relationship with him.

DO ask the Holy Spirit to help you determine what specifically you should focus on, each time you begin to meditate.

DO expect to be transformed as you learn to orient your mind, your heart, and your spirit toward the things of God.

DON'T give up too soon; meditating can feel awkward at first, but with practice it will begin to feel more comfortable

DON'T mix Christian meditation with other types, such as focusing on yourself rather than God, and expect the same result.

Spend Quiet Times with God

The demands and distractions of life in twenty-first-century America are well known. What is less known, it seems, is that you can subdue those demands and distractions and find your way back to a saner way of living. More important, in the process you can grow closer to God. But it takes an intentional effort.

Spending "quiet time" with God used to be a daily activity in a Christian's life. Many Christians still do enjoy a special time with God each day, but many others have dropped the practice entirely. And others believe that because they are in continual communication with God, they do not need a quiet time.

And yet, the only person who ever lived who had unbroken fellowship with God still spent quiet times with the Father.

That person was Jesus, of course. Of all people, he would seem the least likely to find the need to get away and pray; he wasn't driven to prayer for the same reasons most people are—the need for forgiveness, worry over the stresses of life, fear over what the future holds. Still, Jesus withdrew to the wilderness to spend intentional time in prayer.

If Jesus needed those quiet times with God, how much more do people need those times today, when the noise and clamor and busyness of everyday life drown out not only people's thoughts but also their prayers?

 All He asks is that . . . we spend a while thinking about Him, meditating on Him, talking to Him, listening in silence, occupying ourselves with Him—totally and thoroughly lost in the hiding place of His presence.
—Chuck Swindoll

The number one reason people give for not spending time with God is, well, the lack of time. And yet, people do make time for what they truly want to do. If that is the case, what really keeps people from spending quiet time with God? Here are some possible reasons, from several Christian thinkers:

- *John Donne*—"I throw myself down in my chamber, and I call in and invite God and his angels thither, and when they are there, I neglect God and his angels, for the noise of a fly, for the rattling of a coach, for the whining of a door."

- *G. H. Knight*—"Before I can have any joy in being alone with God I must have learned not to fear being alone with myself . . . shrinking from any deep self-scrutiny."

- *Henri Nouwen*—"When we try to become very still, we often find ourselves so overwhelmed by our noisy inner voices that we can hardly wait to get busy and distracted again. Our

interesting to note

In *Practicing the Presence of God*, Brother Lawrence offered a cure for distraction: think about God all the time. When you "think of Him often, you will find it easy to keep your mind calm in time of prayer, or at least to recall it from its wanderings," he wrote.

As often as possible Jesus withdrew to out-of-the-way places for prayer.

Luke 5:16 MSG

inner life often looks like a banana tree full of jumping monkeys."

- *A. W. Tozer*—"Modern civilization is so complex as to make the devotional life all but impossible. It wears us out by multiplying distractions and beats us down by destroying our solitude."

- *William Wilberforce*—"This perpetual hurry of business and company ruins me in soul if not in body . . . I have been keeping too late hours."

If any of those names are familiar to you, you likely see the irony in their comments. Donne lived at the turn of the seventeenth century, Wilberforce at the turn of the nineteenth, and Knight at the turn of the twentieth. Tozer died in 1963, long before technology made modern civilization even more complex. And though he lived into the mid-1990s, Nouwen experienced a world devoid of the jumping monkeys of cyberspace. Yet those things that interfered with their time with God echo those of contemporary Christians: fear of solitude, annoying sounds, numerous distractions, overwork, and noisy inner voices.

Each of those writers elsewhere affirmed that it was worth the struggle to spend quiet time with God. Whether they read the Bible, prayed, sang, or simply sat in the presence of God, it was time well spent. Another Christian thinker, A. T. Pierson, offered this advice on scheduling your quiet time: "God knows how to save for you the time you sacredly keep for communion with Him." And that is the key: asking God to show you where you can find that elusive time.

what's essential

The need for time alone with God has always been great, but it has never been greater than in this twenty-four/seven culture. The busyness, noise, and activity that dominate contemporary life make it essential for Christians to draw on God's strength in their quiet times with God.

DO set aside specific time to spend with God; planning that time is essential if your schedule is particularly crowded.

DO follow the pattern Jesus set for getting away by himself so he could find strength in his time with God.

DON'T allow your quiet times with God to become so obligatory or routine that you lose the joy of being in God's presence.

DON'T feel guilty if your first attempts at spending a quiet time with God feel awkward; eventually it will likely become second nature to you.

How Do I Grow Closer to God?

PASSION

Let all those who take refuge and put their trust in You rejoice; let them ever sing and shout for joy, because You make a covering over them and defend them; let those also who love Your name be joyful in You and be in high spirits.

Psalm 5:11 AMP

Nothing is so contagious as enthusiasm. It moves stones; it charms brutes.

Edward Bulwer-Lytton

Whenever I get to a low point, I go back to the basics. I ask myself, "Why am I doing this?" It comes down to passion.

Lyn St. James

Trust God in Every Situation

Throughout the Bible, God tells his people to trust him. But trusting him isn't always easy. Just ask Noah, who may have wished God had said, "You have to trust me only when what I tell you to do makes sense." But trusting God no matter what may mean building a boat in the desert.

> Trust in the LORD with all your heart and do not lean on your own understanding. In all your ways acknowledge Him, and He will make your paths straight.
>
> **Proverbs 3:5–6** NASB

Most of the time, trusting God involves placing a situation in God's hands, believing—or trying your best to believe—that he will either change it or give you what you need to endure it. Some situations are easier than others. Trusting God to provide money for groceries, however desperate your situation may be, is just not the same thing as trusting God when you've been diagnosed with inoperable cancer.

Trusting in God when you are in need is the kind of trust the prophet Habakkuk expressed—the kind that can rejoice regardless of the circumstances: "Though the fig tree does not bud and there are no grapes on the vines, though the olive crop fails and the fields produce no food, though there are no sheep in the pen and no cattle in the

> It is a glorious thing to know that your Father God makes no mistakes in directing or permitting that which crosses the path of your life. It is the glory of God to conceal a matter. It is our glory to trust Him, no matter what.
>
> **Joni Eareckson Tada**

stalls, yet I will rejoice in the LORD, I will be joyful in God my Savior" (Habakkuk 3:17–18 NIV).

Trusting God for your very life is the kind of trust David expressed in Psalm 23: "Even though I walk through the valley of the shadow of death, I will fear no evil, for you are with me; your rod and your staff, they comfort me" (v. 4 NIV).

At other times—thankfully, rarely—God requires a different kind of trust. That is when he asks you to step out of your comfort zone, discard every shred of pride you have, take no notice of the friends, family, and neighbors who are mocking you, and do something that appears to border on sheer lunacy.

 God is God. Because He is God, He is worthy of my trust and obedience. I will find rest nowhere but in His holy will, a will that is unspeakably beyond my largest notions of what He is up to.
—Elisabeth Elliot

For Noah, that meant building a boat to prepare for a flood that no one saw coming. For you, there is no telling what it may mean. As E. M. Bounds once wrote, "When all is said and done, there is a sort of risk in faith and its exercise." That certainly applies when God asks you to step out in faith and do something that flies in the face of human reason. When you risk losing everything, including your reputation and good standing in the community, you need to be sure you heard God right. But once you are convinced you did—and you've said yes to God—there's no turning back. Leaving a boat half built would have meant certain destruction for Noah and his family.

What are you trusting God for right now? Take whatever that is, no matter how big or small, possible or impossible, within reach or unattainable, and place it in God's hands. Do whatever it takes to make that action real. Visualize the hands of Jesus closing around the situation you've just handed him, hiding it from your view—or imagine an altogether different way of handing the situation to God, a way that resonates with you and helps you to make the action real and concrete.

Now consider your action to be a training exercise in trust. You have given God a current situation in anticipation of all those difficult situations in the future. He has shielded it from your view. You cannot see what he is doing with it. You must resist the temptation to take the situation back. You must simply trust that he is doing something with it.

To keep your mind occupied with the right things during this time of blind trust, meditate on these Scriptures and others that deal with trust:

- "Those who know your name will trust in you, for you, LORD, have never forsaken those who seek you" (Psalm 9:10 NIV).

- "Our ancestors trusted in you, and you rescued them. They cried out to you and were

interesting to note

One recent Gallup poll revealed that 95 percent of Americans believe in God, a percentage that has held steady for more than three decades. But belief doesn't automatically translate into trust; 80 percent said they believe God answers prayer, while only 60 percent said they trust God completely.

Offer the sacrifices of righteousness, and trust in the LORD.
Psalm 4:5 NASB

saved. They trusted in you and were never disgraced" (Psalm 22:4–5 NLT).

What is the point? The point is preparation—preparing to trust God when he asks you to do something outlandish. And he just may.

what's essential

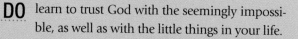

Evangelist Rick Joyner once said, "If the Lord created the world out of chaos, He can easily deal with any problem that we have." Take that sentiment to heart. No situation in your life is too big, too complicated, or too messy for God to handle.

DO learn to trust God with the seemingly impossible, as well as with the little things in your life.

DO build up a treasury of situations in which you've trusted God completely, in preparation for more difficult situations ahead.

DON'T expect everything God asks you to do to make sense according to your limited understanding.

DON'T give in to the temptation to take back something you've turned over to God; trust him for the patience to wait for him to act.

Talk Things Over with God

Everyone knows what a conversation is. It is a back-and-forth exchange that involves both talking and listening. There is little difference between a conversation and a prayer—except that the back-and-forth exchange is with the Creator of the universe. That makes it a big difference, and one that often complicates the conversation.

Y ou were created to be in a relationship with God, but it wouldn't be much of a relationship if the two of you never talked to each other. Neither would it be much of a relationship if you did all the talking. Imagine having a relationship like that with a mere mortal. It certainly wouldn't last long.

Jesus called his followers "friends"—and if you are one of his followers, that makes you one of his friends as well. Do you talk to your friends? Of course. Do you listen to them? Of course you do. They are your friends. And because Jesus is your friend, you need to talk to him, and listen to him, as well.

British-born pastor and theologian George Buttrick, who served as pastor of a Presbyterian church

> Don't fret or worry. Instead of worrying, pray. Let petitions and praises shape your worries into prayers, letting God know your concerns.
> **Philippians 4:6 MSG**

> The trouble with nearly everybody who prays is that he says "Amen" and runs away before God has a chance to reply. Listening to God is far more important than giving Him your ideas.
> **Frank Laubach**

in New York City for more than fifty years, wrote this in his 1942 book, *Prayer*: "*Prayer* is listening, as well as speaking, receiving as well as asking; and its deepest mood is friendship held in reverence." If you have trouble imagining Jesus as a friend, think of your relationship as a "friendship held in reverence."

The same concept applies to God the Father. Jesus called him *Abba*, a familiar term akin to *Daddy*. Some Christians have no trouble praying to "Daddy," but if you are not one of them, think of God the Father as a warm, loving dad for whom you have great respect.

Don't pray when you feel like it; make an appointment with the King and keep it.
—Corrie ten Boom

The point is, there is no need to elevate your conversation with God to a formal, artificial level. If you grew up in a tradition in which prayers rang from the pulpit in proper Elizabethan style, you may feel compelled to try to duplicate that. But God wants to hear the cry of your heart. Old Testament prayers should reassure you of this. "Why did you bring us across the Jordan River if you are going to let the Amorites kill us?" Joshua asked God (Joshua 7:7 NLT). He challenged God's leading and by inference accused him of bringing about their destruction. He prayed the cry of his heart with little concern about getting the words just right.

But maybe you've got the talking part down. You have no problem talking to God in a way that feels natural to you. What about the listening part, though? How does God speak to you—and when? He doesn't always speak while you are praying, and he doesn't necessarily speak in an audible voice.

- God speaks through your conscience. You may receive sudden insight or a strong impression about something God wants you to do.

- God speaks through the Bible. You may find the answer to a concern you are praying about right in the pages of Scripture. That is God speaking to you as the Holy Spirit directs you to a certain passage and illuminates its meaning for you (John 14:16–17; Ephesians 1:17).

- God speaks audibly, sometimes in a whisper (1 Kings 19:12), sometimes from behind you (Isaiah 30:21), sometimes in the night (1 Samuel 3:2–10).

As with any direction you sense, remember to compare what you "hear" with the Scriptures, following the lead of the Bereans, who "searched the Scriptures daily to find out whether these things were so" (Acts 17:11 NKJV). What God says to you in prayer will not contradict what he says to you in the Bible.

interesting to note

Listening requires silence, and many people today are uncomfortable with that. In a less frenetic time, it was common practice to spend several minutes in silent prayer about one thing before praying about the next thing, listening attentively for God to speak during those moments of silence.

I say to you, whatever things you ask when you pray, believe that you receive them, and you will have them.

Mark 11:24 NKJV

You can have further assurance that you are hearing from God by remembering the biblical analogy of the sheep and the shepherd (John 10:4–5). The sheep in a particular flock recognize the voice of their master—and not that of a stranger who would lead them astray.

what's essential

Jeremiah 33:3 says this: "Call to Me, and I will answer you, and show you great and mighty things, which you do not know" (NKJV). That is God's assurance to you that when you call on him in prayer, he will answer you, and he will reveal "great and mighty things" to you.

DO remember that prayer is simply a conversation—with the Creator of the universe, yes, but also with a friend.

DO listen for an answer from God, which may come as a strong sensation in your conscience or an audible voice.

DON'T wait until you feel like praying to pray; just start praying and don't focus on your feelings.

DON'T forget to compare what you hear with what the Bible says; his spoken word will never contradict his written Word.

Rely on the Spirit's Guidance

Some days are just too hard. Too many decisions, too much to do, too much to think about—wouldn't you just love to have someone come along and take charge? Well, all you have to do is ask. One of the Holy Spirit's functions is to guide those who have placed their trust in God.

While they were worshiping the Lord and fasting, the Holy Spirit said, Separate now for Me Barnabas and Saul for the work to which I have called them.

Acts 13:2 AMP

In the corporate world, having a personal assistant is a must for executives, managers, and certain other staffers. Personal assistants make sure you know where you are supposed to be and what you need with you now, plus where you need to be tomorrow and the next day and well into the future.

Now imagine having someone in your personal life who performs a similar function. One difference—and this is a major difference—is that you are not the one calling the shots. You do not tell the Holy Spirit what your schedule is and simply expect him to keep track of it. No, the Holy Spirit knows what you should be doing, and your job is to follow his leading.

The guidance of the Spirit is generally by gentle suggestions or drawings, and not in violent pushes; and it requires great childlikeness of heart to be faithful to it. The secret of being made willing lies in a definite giving up of our will.

Hannah Whitall Smith

Why is this so important? You've probably done pretty well on your own. But imagine what you've been missing! Jesus promises you a life of abundance, and the Holy Spirit can lead you right into it. And the Holy Spirit can keep you out of a whole lot of potential danger and trouble.

But the Spirit doesn't lead just anyone. The Bible makes it clear that those whom the Spirit leads are children of God (Romans 8:14) who are no longer under the law of Moses (Galatians 5:18). Sound like you? Great! Now that you know you can be led by the Spirit, it is important to know how the Spirit will lead you.

I seek the will of the Spirit of God through, or in connection with, the Word of God. The Spirit and the Word must be combined. If I look to the Spirit alone without the Word, I lay myself open to great delusions. If the Holy Spirit leads us, He will do it according to the Scriptures and never contrary to them.
—George Müller

The first thing that is important to know is that the Holy Spirit will never lead you in the wrong direction. John calls him the "Spirit of truth," who will "guide you into all truth. He will not speak on his own; he will speak only what he hears, and he will tell you what is yet to come" (John 16:13 NIV).

The next thing you need to know is that the Holy Spirit leads you in two primary ways: externally, through the Bible; and internally, through his indwelling presence in your life.

The Spirit's leading through the Bible. Ephesians 6:17 calls the Bible the "sword of the Spirit" (NIV). It is through the Word that the Spirit pierces your heart and lets you know when you've done wrong, prompting you to confess your sin to God and make things right with him. The Spirit also illuminates the Bible, giving you a decided edge over the unspiritual person, who "can't receive the gifts of God's Spirit. There's no capacity for them. They seem like so much silliness. Spirit can be known only by spirit—God's Spirit and our spirits in open communion" (1 Corinthians 2:14 MSG).

The Spirit also revealed to the apostles the truth of the Scriptures, which they then preached to the rest of the church (1 Corinthians 2:9–13). Paul wrote: "This is what we speak, not in words taught us by human wisdom but in words taught by the Spirit, expressing spiritual truths in spiritual words" (v. 13 NIV).

The Spirit's leading through his presence. The Holy Spirit's power is at work in you (Ephesians 3:20), strengthening you (Ephesians 3:16) and enabling you to resist wrongdoing (Ephesians 6:13). The Spirit lives in you (Romans 8:11) and leads you (Romans 8:14).

The Spirit also actively participates in your prayer life, which is another way he directs you:

"When we see through a glass darkly, the Spirit adjusts and fo-
cuses what we are asking until it corresponds to the will of God,"
Richard Foster wrote in his 1992 book, *Prayer*.

If you want someone to take charge of your life and lead you in
the way you should go, you cannot do better than the Holy Spirit.

what's essential

Sometimes it will seem hard to know how the Spirit is
leading you. In those situations, seek the counsel of
other mature Christians and act on what you believe
to be the Spirit's direction. God will honor your efforts
to know his will.

DO expect the Holy Spirit to speak to you through
the Bible.

DO realize that the Spirit strengthens you and
leads you in the way you should go.

DON'T forget to compare what you believe is the
leading of the Spirit to what the Bible has to
say.

DON'T act first and then ask the Spirit's blessing; the
Spirit sets the agenda, and you determine
whether or not you will obey.

Fast—and Hold Fast

Fasting isn't a popular subject these days. Americans love to eat, and American Christians are no exception to that. In fact, fellowship around the table is a hallmark of church life. The early Christians set that pattern—but they also set the pattern for abstaining from food, and for good reason.

Fasting as a spiritual practice exists in many cultures and among many faiths. The Christian practice stems from the Jewish custom of fasting in observance of a holy day or as a sign of mourning or repentance. At times the Jews abstained from food entirely; at other times they fasted as Daniel did, on vegetables and water (Daniel 10:2–3).

Specific occasions for fasting in the Jewish Scriptures include Esther's call for the Jews to observe a three-day fast before she pleaded their case before King Ahasuerus (Esther 4:16); a seven-day fast following the death of Saul (1 Chronicles 10:12); and David's fast on behalf of his dying son (2 Samuel 12:16). Many other examples are found throughout the Old Testament.

When you fast, don't put on a sad face like the hypocrites. They make their faces look sad to show people they are fasting. I tell you the truth, those hypocrites already have their full reward. So when you fast, comb your hair and wash your face.

Matthew 6:16–17 NCV

Fasting must not be confined to the question of food and drink; fasting should really be made to include abstinence from anything which is legitimate in and of itself for the sake of some special spiritual purpose.

Martyn Lloyd-Jones

Jesus, of course, went entirely without food for forty days (Matthew 4:1–2), echoing Moses' forty-day fast in the wilderness (Deuteronomy 9:18). Paul was so overcome by his encounter with the Lord that he fasted for three days (Acts 9:9). The early Christians continued the practice and fasted before they consecrated Paul and Barnabas for service (Acts 13:3).

 Fasting confirms our utter dependence upon God by finding in Him a source of sustenance beyond food.
—Dallas Willard

So there is a lot of evidence of fasting in the Judeo-Christian tradition, but what does that have to do with you today? Why is fasting essential to your life with God? For one thing, if you want to draw closer to God, fasting is one of the best ways to accomplish that. Here's why:

- By eliminating your dependence on food, you learn to depend on God for true sustenance.

- You are free to focus on God and spend time with him when you remove meal planning, cooking, eating, and cleaning the kitchen from your day's schedule.

- You allow the Holy Spirit to reveal aspects of your character and your way of thinking, such as your priorities.

- Self-denial promotes self-control, a fruit of the Spirit (Galatians 5:23).

- Fasting clarifies your thinking and sharpens your senses—and your sensitivity to the leading of the Holy Spirit.

- Reducing your food intake enables you to share in a small way in the suffering of the malnourished and the poor, the "least of these" (Matthew 25:40 NKJV) for whom Jesus had such compassion.

- Denying yourself something you enjoy can renew your gratitude toward God for all he has given you.

And those are just some of the spiritual benefits. The health benefits are equally numerous.

At the heart of fasting is denying yourself something you ordinarily depend on. While that most often means food, you can apply the concept of fasting to anything that needs to be temporarily removed from center stage in your life. "Fasting can be a painful admission that I am not free, that my life is enslaved, obsessed or addicted to external things such as food, drink, codependent relationships, sex, television, privacy and the like," wrote Franciscan priest Albert Haase. Your list may look entirely different.

No matter what your reason for fasting, Jesus warned against making a show of it (Matthew 6:16–18). That is not to say that you shouldn't explain yourself when you decline someone's offer of food; Jesus was speaking specifically about those who took great pride in the huge sacrifice they made when they fasted. Fasting is to be a sign of obedience, not religious superiority.

interesting to note

The *Didache*, a handbook for the early church, advised Christians to fast only on Wednesdays and Fridays, so they wouldn't be confused with the "hypocrites" (the Pharisees), who fasted on Mondays and Thursdays. Fasting two days a week was a given; Christians needed only to be told when to fast.

Is this not the fast that I have chosen: To loose the bonds of wickedness, to undo the heavy burdens, to let the oppressed go free, and that you break every yoke?
Isaiah 58:6 NKJV

There's no question that fasting isn't easy amid American abundance. Food is all around you, and your awareness of that will likely increase as your food intake decreases. Fasting requires tenacity, holding fast to God to see this through. But that is just fine, because that is why you are fasting—to draw closer to God and remain in his presence.

what's essential

In simplest terms, fasting is prioritizing. Fasting indicates you have placed a greater priority on spending time with God than anything else, for a given period of time—even if it means giving up meals, entertainment, sports, or other activities that would divert your time and attention from the Lord.

DO seek medical counsel before beginning an extended fast, especially if you have diabetes or another physical disorder.

DO seek the Holy Spirit's guidance on what you should abstain from and how long you should fast.

DON'T fast simply for the sake of fasting and expect to draw closer to God. A spiritual fast is intentional and Spirit-led.

DON'T limit your thinking about fasting to food alone; consider fasting from anything that consumes too much of your time and attention.

Serve the Lord Joyfully

David is the biblical character most often associated with joyfully serving the Lord, particularly in a congregation. But another character—this one a judge, a prophet, and a military leader—is an example of joyful service at work and in everyday life. The name of this servant of God? Deborah.

Make a joyful noise to the Lord, all you lands! Serve the Lord with gladness! Come before His presence with singing!
Psalm 100:1–2 AMP

Unlike her male counterparts who settled disputes at the gates of Jerusalem, Deborah held court in the shade of a palm tree in Ephraim. As a judge, she was held in high esteem by both men and women and performed a function normally reserved for men. Her story is told in Judges 4 and 5, at a time of chaos for the nation of Israel. The Israelites couldn't seem to get it together; they were supposed to rule over the land of the Canaanites, but they had been living under the thumb of Jabin, Canaan's king, and Sisera, his military commander, for twenty years. They cried out to the Lord to be free of their oppressors.

But it took Deborah to hear God, take him at his word, and obey his command. It was time, she told Barak, Israel's military commander, to

Blessed the man and woman who are able to serve cheerfully in the second rank— a big test.
Mary Slessor

rout the Canaanites and retake the land God had given them. Barak's reply was along the lines of "Well, all right, if you insist, but you have to go with me." That was fine with Deborah and part of her strategy all along.

Deborah's battle plan, which she credited to God, worked exactly as she said it would. *The Message* puts the final outcome this way: "The People of Israel pressed harder and harder on Jabin king of Canaan until there was nothing left of him" (Judges 4:24). Another outcome? Deborah's action resulted in forty years of peace for the Israelites.

 What is it to serve God and to do His will? Nothing else than to show mercy to our neighbor. For it is our neighbor who needs our service; God in heaven needs it not.
—Martin Luther

Deborah served God by listening to him, trusting him, and taking action when it appeared no one else would—and at a time when the Israelites were outmanned and "outweaponed" to a considerable degree. Hers was not mere lip service; hers was service in action. But what about the "joyful" part?

Judges 5 takes care of that. The entire chapter—believed, by the way, to be one of the oldest portions of the Bible as well as one of the earliest examples of Hebrew poetry—recounts this portion of Israel's history in a joyful song sung by Deborah and Barak. It is a song of praise to God and gratitude to the people of Israel for rallying around a cause that seemed destined to fail.

One of the most striking aspects of this story is Deborah's resolve. Her conviction that this was God's plan and her faith in him to bring it to fruition never wavered. While the rest of Israel moaned and groaned over Jabin's oppression, Deborah remained attentive to God and "set [her] face like flint" (Isaiah 50:7 NASB), determined to do God's will.

Then she broke out into song. The joy that she had to hold back in the heat of battle came gushing forth; she couldn't contain it any longer.

This is service: to serve God and people by doing what God wants you to do, with complete trust, without complaint, and with a joyful attitude. If it means getting your hands dirty—going to the battlefield when you could just stay in the shade of your palm tree—so be it. To update the image a bit, Martin Luther King Jr. said this: "Anybody can serve. You do not have to have a college degree to serve. You do not have to make your subject and verb agree to serve. You only need a heart full of grace, a soul generated by love."

interesting to note

One Hebrew word for *worship (avah)* can also mean "service," and it is a word David used in some of his psalms, particularly Psalm 100, where verse 2 can be translated "Worship the LORD with gladness" or "Serve the LORD with gladness." The two concepts were also linked with manual labor.

The master answered, "You did well. You are a good and loyal servant. Because you were loyal with small things, I will let you care for much greater things. Come and share my joy with me."
Matthew 25:21 NCV

Age is no excuse; gender is no excuse. Look at it this way: if you make sure your soul has been generated by love and your heart is full of grace, joyful service cannot help but be a natural result.

what's essential

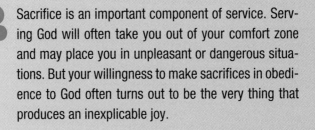

Sacrifice is an important component of service. Serving God will often take you out of your comfort zone and may place you in unpleasant or dangerous situations. But your willingness to make sacrifices in obedience to God often turns out to be the very thing that produces an inexplicable joy.

DO examine your heart to determine whether you are serving God joyfully or out of obligation.

DO serve God by listening for his voice, trusting what he says, and acting on what you've heard.

DON'T let the overwhelming odds against you stop you from obeying what you know God has told you to do.

DON'T let your situation in life—such as Deborah's gender in a male-dominated culture—prevent you from serving God.

How Do I Grow Closer to God?

CONTENTMENT

My choice is you, GOD, first and only. And now I find I'm your choice! You set me up with a house and yard. And then you made me your heir! The wise counsel GOD gives when I'm awake is confirmed by my sleeping heart. Day and night I'll stick with GOD; I've got a good thing going and I'm not letting go.

Psalm 16:5–8 MSG

Contentment is a pearl of great price, and whoever procures it at the expense of ten thousand desires makes a wise and a happy purchase.

John Balguy

When the heart is content to be without the outward blessing, it is as happy as it would be with it, for it is at rest.

Charles Spurgeon

Allow for God's Surprises

A priest loses his ability to talk for months on end. A prophet of God is told to marry a prostitute. Two men mourning the death of the supposed Messiah meet a stranger who turns out to be the Messiah. As dissimilar as these events are, all are acts of God—a God of surprises.

Zechariah, Hosea, and the two disciples walking to Emmaus had this in common: each had God neatly wrapped up in a box of predictable dimensions. But God broke out of those dimensions and caught them off guard by doing something totally unexpected. At the appointed moment, God dismantled their preconceptions about him and began doing a new thing.

For Zechariah, who had faithfully served God in the temple his entire life, that "new thing" was the pregnancy of his wife, Elizabeth, who was "well along in years" (Luke 1:18 NIV). For all of Zechariah's faithful service, God still managed to stun him by showing up in an astonishing way to deliver a miraculous message—one that

Zechariah had a hard time believing. For that, his ability to speak was taken away for the duration of the pregnancy (v. 20).

For Hosea, who had also faithfully served God, the news had to be dismaying at best. The Lord wanted him—a man of God, no less!—to marry a woman who would immediately begin to prostitute herself out to other men. Granted, this unusual marriage was to serve as a blatant representation of the dysfunctional relationship between God and faithless Israel. But really—this was hardly the perk Hosea expected in return for his loyalty and commitment to God.

 If you can see the path laid out in front of you, step by step—it's not your path.
—Joseph Campbell

For the two men headed for Emmaus, the day's events had been bewildering. Jesus had been crucified three days earlier, and they just heard that the heavily guarded tomb in which his body had been placed was now empty. A stranger met them on the road and began discussing biblical prophecy. Over dinner, the men suddenly recognized their new companion—Jesus, the Messiah. And then they knew where his body was (Luke 24).

Has God ever caught you off guard? Has he ever done something so different from what you expected that you wondered if he was even involved? Even if your answer to those questions is no, here's a question nearly everyone can answer yes to: have you ever questioned what God supposedly told someone else to do simply because it did not sound like something God would do?

The God you serve is a God of astonishing activity, a God of surprises. For millennia, his followers have tried to train him to behave in a predictable way; a tame, domesticated God is much easier to understand than one who tells a no-nonsense fisherman to get out of his boat and take a walk on a stormy sea. But God will have none of that. "You thought that I was just like you," God told his people (Psalm 50:21 NASB), and then he proceeded to set them straight.

God continues to set people straight about how different and unpredictable he is. You only have to look around at your fellow believers to find surprises at every turn: *God called him to be a pastor? So now she claims to be born again?* "If ever I reach heaven, I expect to find three wonders there: first, to meet some I had not thought to see there; second, to miss some I had expected to see there; and third—the greatest wonder of all—to find myself there," John Newton, who wrote the lyrics to "Amazing Grace," once maintained.

God can do what he wants, when he wants, and how he wants, and that can be unsettling to people who think they have him figured out. But he is, after all, a God of wonder, awe, and amazement, and his surprises should come as no surprise at all.

what's essential

The early Christians lived in a state of continual expectation, looking for the return of Jesus at any moment. Continual expectation is not a bad state to live in, always prepared to see God intervene in human life in ways that jostle his followers' preconceptions about how he behaves.

DO expect the God of wonder to continue to surprise you throughout your life.

DO read the Bible with a sharpened awareness of incidents in which God surprised his followers —and his enemies.

DON'T keep God in whatever box you may have placed him in; let God be God in your life— untamed, undomesticated, unpredictable.

DON'T discount the possibility of God's acting in unusual ways in the lives of those around you.

Set Aside Time for Worship

In some churches today, worship has become so closely associated with singing that the true meaning of worship has been largely lost. Far from being confined to the "praise and worship" portion of a church service, true worship is something a believer can do anytime, anywhere, alone or with other Christians.

In ancient Israel, six tribes were instructed to worship on Mount Gerizim while the other six were to worship on Mount Ebal. The temple on Mount Gerizim was eventually destroyed, and had it not been for a brief incident hundreds of years later, Mount Gerizim would have faded into obscurity. But in the intervening years, the Samaritans, whom the Jews hated, took over that location as the site of their worship.

So when Jesus engaged a Samaritan woman in conversation—considered a scandalous act at the time—she recognized him as a prophet but challenged the Jews' assertion that true worship could take place only in Jerusalem and not on Mount Gerizim. Jesus' reply to her changed the concept of worship for millennia to come: "Woman,

Come, let us worship and bow down. Let us kneel before the LORD our maker, for he is our God. We are the people he watches over, the flock under his care. If only you would listen to his voice today!

Psalm 95:6–7 NLT

All of history is moving toward one great goal, the white-hot worship of God and his Son among all the peoples of the earth.

John Piper

believe Me, the hour is coming when you will neither on this mountain, nor in Jerusalem, worship the Father. You worship what you do not know; we know what we worship, for salvation is of the Jews. But the hour is coming, and now is, when the true worshipers will worship the Father in spirit and truth; for the Father is seeking such to worship Him. God is Spirit, and those who worship Him must worship in spirit and truth" (John 4:21–24 NKJV).

This was a radical concept. People worshiped at altars and temples and other sacred sites. To suggest that people would no longer worship the Father on Mount Gerizim was preposterous; to suggest they would cease to worship in Jerusalem bordered on blasphemous.

 Christian worship is alive because, in its essence, it is a conversation between two living realities—the one true, eternal God and the body of Christ, the church.
—Gary A. Furr

But Jesus did not stop there and leave her wondering what on earth he meant. He continued, telling her that the time was coming when people would worship the Father in spirit and in truth—no doubt still leaving her wondering what on earth he meant. Weren't they already worshiping in spirit—to her understanding, worshiping from the heart—and in the revealed truth about God?

Obviously, this Jesus was talking about something entirely different, and her reply indicates she's content to wait for the Messiah to come and reveal whatever this prophet was talking about. Little did she know that she was sitting right next to the Messiah.

So if the people were already worshiping God in their understanding of "spirit and truth," what did Jesus mean? And what does this mean for your worship of God today?

There's little question that Jesus was referring to the abandonment of the trappings that had characterized Jewish worship to that point, such as special vestments, feast days, incense, lamp stands, animal sacrifices, and so forth. This new kind of worship would be more closely attuned to God's nature—spiritual in nature rather than physical, replacing those trappings with concepts like the spiritual nature of the body of Christ, the priesthood of all believers, the sacrifices of praise and service.

But what about truth? If the Jews were already worshiping in truth, what would replace their wor-ship? Biblical scholars generally agree that most of the Old Testament foreshadowed the coming of Christ; the truth revealed in the Old Testament foreshadowed the reality that would be revealed with the coming of Christ as the Messiah. Believ-ers would now worship God in the light of the revealed truth about Christ.

What all this means for you is this: whether you are driving in your car, resting on your bed, hiking through the woods, or sitting in a church pew, your worship in spirit and in truth is pleasing to God. Worship is an attitude—of adoration, gratitude, awe, wonder, and much more—toward God, not the singing portion of a church service.

what's essential

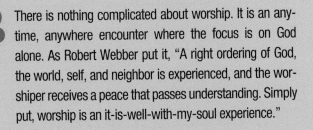There is nothing complicated about worship. It is an any-time, anywhere encounter where the focus is on God alone. As Robert Webber put it, "A right ordering of God, the world, self, and neighbor is experienced, and the worshiper receives a peace that passes understanding. Simply put, worship is an it-is-well-with-my-soul experience."

DO worship God in spirit—according to God's nature—and in truth—according to the revealed truth about Jesus Christ.

DO remember that worship is not confined to Sunday mornings but occurs whenever you fix your focus on God in adoration.

DON'T complicate worship by thinking you need to feel a certain way or be in a certain environment to truly worship.

DON'T miss an opportunity to ask the Lord to explain something to you, as the Samaritan woman did.

Pursue a Life of Holiness

Holiness? Who even thinks about holiness anymore? God, for one. He told his people to be holy because he is holy. Holiness is not a concept reserved for saints. You can become holy, and you can find lots of ways to achieve holiness. And there is only one steadfast rule: do not try to be holy.

William Law was an eighteenth-century curate who later became a spiritual director and a well-known author in his time. Two of his books, *A Serious Call to a Devout and Holy Life* and *A Practical Treatise upon Christian Perfection*, had a profound effect on the likes of Andrew Murray, John and Charles Wesley, George Whitefield, William Wilberforce, and Samuel Johnson, who credited reading *Serious Call* with providing the first step toward his devotion to Christ. Despite Law's influence, his mystical bent kept him banned from both the pulpit and secular halls.

Among his many beliefs on what constitutes a holy life, one in particular would earn him a welcome mat in both sacred and secular venues today. He believed all of life is holy: "As a good Christian should consider every place as holy, because God is there, so he should look upon every part of his life as a matter of holiness, because it is offered unto God. The profession of a clergyman is a holy profession, because it is a ministration in holy things, an attendance at the altar. But worldly business is to be made holy unto the Lord, by being done as a service unto Him, and in conformity to His Divine will."

The professional clergy at the time may have appreciated his view of the clergy but not so much his elevation of all of life to the same status. To Law, the very definition of Christianity meant universal holiness in every aspect of life, including a willingness to not shun the world but to turn "all worldly enjoyments into means of piety and devotion to God."

We should not think that holiness is based on what we do but rather on what we are, for it is not our works which sanctify us but we who sanctify our works.
—Meister Eckehart

Holiness, however, should not be the focus of the Christian's life; it should be the fruit of a life wholly devoted to God. Even Oswald Chambers, who called holiness "the chief end of man," agreed that striving to achieve holiness was futile.

While many elements factor into holiness, the following three are essential.

- *Prayer and devotion.* When writers from an earlier time used the word *devotion,* they weren't referring to the often brief sessions with God that are known today as "devotions," daily or otherwise. They meant sheer, utter, complete abandonment to God. French cleric and author Jean N. Grou called it "a fixed, enduring habit of mind permeating the whole life and shaping every action." That habit of mind involved private prayer and lots of it. Without exception, holiness writers considered prayer and devotion to be indispensable to a holy life.

- *Humility.* Christian humility is a recognition that your talents and accomplishments are due to God's working through you and not due to anything within yourself. Poet John Donne considered humility to be the groundwork for holiness; a person who lacked humility, he believed, could listen to sermons all day, read the Bible all night, and still miss hearing the voice of God.

- *Obedience.* Missionary Florence Allshorn also saw holiness as a result of a life devoted to God and not something Christians should pursue. "So long as our eyes are on our own personal whiteness as an end in itself, the thing breaks down," she wrote in her journal. "God can do

nothing while my interest is in my own personal character—
He will take care of this if I obey His call."

God has little use for outward attempts at holiness based on
a rigid set of rules. What God wants, and has always wanted, is
for his people to devote themselves to prayer, in an attitude of
humility and obedience. That is the essence of holiness.

what's essential

If you allow it to, holiness can seep into every corner of your life—your friendships, your home life, your job, your recreation, your church life. When you humble yourself before God and devote your life to prayer and obedience, holiness will naturally follow.

DO recognize holiness as an attribute that is both desirable and attainable, even in the twenty-first century.

DO become aware of the many references to holiness in the Bible.

DON'T focus your attention on becoming holy; let holiness result from your life with God.

DON'T think of holiness in terms of a rigid set of rules controlling your appearance and behavior; throw out the rules and obey God instead.

Learn to Forgive

Learning to forgive is among the most valuable of all of life's lessons. Why? Because in forgiving others, you turn the universe on its head; you defy the course of human nature by opting instead for a supernatural act of grace. And as if that is not enough, you reward yourself with the gift of peace.

Be gentle and forbearing with one another and, if one has a difference (a grievance or complaint) against another, readily pardoning each other; even as the Lord has [freely] forgiven you, so must you also [forgive].

Colossians 3:13 AMP

Forgiveness is also among the clearest concepts in the Bible. God extends his forgiveness to you, and you in turn are expected to extend forgiveness to others—and when you do, forgiveness continues to flow from God back to you. What could be simpler than that? Although it is an easy concept to understand, it is not always easy to put it into practice.

The typical human response to an offense is often the desire for retaliation or revenge, or for some manner of misfortune to befall the offender. Finding the high road—the path of forgiveness—can be exceedingly difficult when someone has hurt you. But your willingness to travel that higher road puts you in a place where you can truly forgive.

Forgiveness is love practiced among people who love poorly. It sets us free without wanting anything in return.

Henri Nouwen

On the path of forgiveness, you can expect to learn a bit more about what forgiveness is and what it isn't. Forgiving others is an act of the will and an act of obedience to God; it is not a function of your emotions. You may not feel like forgiving the person who hurt you, but warding off the negative and prolonged effects of harboring unforgiveness is much more important than your fleeting feelings. In time, you just may develop a compassionate heart toward your offender. Even if you don't, you will have rid yourself of the heavy burden of carrying around an unforgiving heart.

 Whoever is devoid of the power to forgive is devoid of the power to love.
—Martin Luther King Jr.

That's all well and good, but here's where many people give up on forgiveness completely: the next step, the step of reconciliation. What so many hurting people fail to realize is that forgiveness is frequently a one-way street between you and the one you need to forgive; it is not always a two-way path that leads to reconciliation. In some cases, reconciliation is unwise to pursue or impossible to accomplish. An abused spouse would be foolish to return to a threatening and dangerous mate; the person you need to forgive may have died or dropped out of sight. Furthermore, you cannot force another person to reconcile with you. Reconciliation is a goal of forgiveness—not a prerequisite for it.

Forgiveness rewards you with the blessing of peace of mind; it does not reward your offender with a license to continue hurting you. Genuinely forgiving another person allows God to come in and replace the pain with the peace that he alone can offer. The Bible tells you to forgive, but it also warns you to "guard your heart" (Proverbs 4:23 NIV). Release your offender to God, and guard yourself against future pain.

While you are extending forgiveness to others, don't forget the importance of forgiving yourself, for everything from a serious breach of confidence to a misguided comment you made in passing. People are often much harder on themselves than others are; if you are in the habit of beating yourself up for every little and big offense, it is time to turn your forgiving heart inward.

But how do you forgive yourself? It helps to remember that God has already forgiven you, and it would be wise to follow his lead. It also helps to imagine a loving God withholding his forgiveness for the things you find yourself fretting about; if you have a healthy concept of who God is, you will likely find that image amusing.

Be kind to one another, tenderhearted, forgiving one another, even as God in Christ forgave you.
Ephesians 4:32 NKJV

God wants his followers to be a forgiving people, and he freely grants them the power to forgive others. But there is a learning curve involved, because an understanding of forgiveness doesn't come naturally. Learn about forgiveness, and learn to forgive. This one lesson will affect every relationship in your life, for the rest of your life. That is a good enough reason to begin practicing forgiveness toward others right now.

what's essential

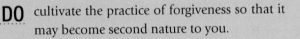

Think about what holds you back from forgiving someone who has wronged you. Compare that obstacle with the rewards that come from pleasing God, releasing your offender to him, and relieving yourself of the burden of unforgiveness. Ask God to replace the obstacle with a forgiving spirit.

DO cultivate the practice of forgiveness so that it may become second nature to you.

DO learn to forgive yourself, no matter what you have done—in recent memory or in the distant past.

DON'T confuse forgiveness and reconciliation; forgiveness is always possible, but reconciliation may not be.

DON'T qualify your forgiveness of others by adding conditions to it; instead extend forgiveness unconditionally.

Face the Future Fearlessly

You do not have to go far to find something to be afraid of. Fear is as close as your television, radio, or Internet connection. Whether it is the latest economic crisis, the spread of a deadly pandemic, or any number of other real or imagined threats, the message is clear: Be afraid. Be very afraid.

Fear serves a purpose. In *The Gift of Fear*, Gavin De Becker, an authority on violent crimes, reminds readers that legitimate fear serves to alert potential victims to danger. To be sure, when the hairs on the back of your neck stand up, you probably need to pay attention and flee the situation. And there is another legitimate form of fear: the fear of the Lord. Whenever that phrase appears in the Bible, God is reminding his people that they need to treat him with awe and respect.

There's also a fleeting fear, the kind that comes over you when you are asked to give a presentation at work or your annual dental checkup is looming. God cares about those temporary fears, of course, and he'll see you through those situations when you turn them over to him.

But the kind of fear you need to vehemently resist is the paralyzing fear that threatens to wreck your life and your relationship with God—because a crippling fear that dominates your life is rooted in a lack of trust in God. Some people would dispute that, claiming that they do trust God but cannot help feeling afraid. Nevertheless, the biblical evidence to the contrary is overwhelming. When the people of God placed their trust in him, they were emboldened to accomplish things they never thought possible.

 Courage is contagious. When a brave man takes a stand, the spines of others are often stiffened.
—Billy Graham

The early church is a case in point. The cowering disciples who feared for their lives when Jesus was crucified were transformed into courageous apostles who defied entire governments and Jewish religious leaders who wanted nothing less than to see them and their movement dead. There is simply no other explanation for their transformation; the Spirit of God came upon them, and they faced persecution and the threat of annihilation with an otherwise inexplicable boldness.

One of the thorniest problems for Christians who fall prey to fear is that fear can grow into a cycle of distrust. A failure to trust God completely makes you vulnerable to fear, and giving in to the fear causes you to doubt God even more. Fear continues to erode whatever trust you once had in God.

You can break that cycle, though—and you must if you want to have a healthy relationship with God that is based on faith in his protection and confidence in his promises. In *The Journey*, Billy Graham reminded Christians that "fear can banish faith, but faith can banish fear." He offered these steps in dealing with fear and restoring your trust in God:

- Turn your fears and worries over to Christ. Neither deny them nor cling to them. Ask Jesus to lift the burden of fear from you.

- Believe the Bible. "Fear vanishes when it is exposed to the promises of God's Word," Graham wrote.

- Pray without ceasing—and pray in faith. Follow Paul's advice in Philippians 4:6–7: "Do not be anxious about anything, but in everything, by prayer and petition, with thanksgiving, present your requests to God. And the peace of God, which transcends all understanding, will guard your hearts and your minds in Christ Jesus" (NIV).

- Pray for strength to endure the situation.

- Pray for wisdom to know what you should do, if anything.

- Ask God to change your circumstances, if it is his will.

And of course, pray for God to help you get rid of the fear that is interfering with a trusting relationship with him.

Freedom from chronic fear is possible, but only if you cooperate with God in availing yourself of the freedom he offers. Let God control the situation—and allow his peace to overcome your fear.

what's essential

When your character reflects fearlessness, people will see that your trust in God is rooted in a bold and grounded confidence. Every time you refuse to allow fear to overwhelm you, you are letting the world around you know that you serve a God who can be trusted.

 DO turn to God immediately when you sense a spirit of fear coming over you.

 DO believe that when you give your fears over to God in prayer, his indescribable peace will replace the worry and anxiety that permeate your life.

 DON'T allow fear to rob you of the abundant life Jesus promised to give you (John 10:10).

 DON'T let fear keep you from doing God's will; obediently do whatever he asks of you, even if you have not yet conquered your fear of doing it.

How Do I Grow Closer to God?

GRACE

A day in Your courts is better than a thousand. I would rather be a door-keeper in the house of my God than dwell in the tents of wicked-ness. For the LORD God is a sun and shield; the LORD will give grace and glory; no good thing will He withhold from those who walk uprightly. O LORD of hosts, blessed is the man who trusts in You!

Psalm 84:10–12 NKJV

Grace means the free, unmer-ited, unexpected love of God, and all the benefits, delights, and comforts which flow from it. It means that while we were sinners and enemies we have been treated as sons and heirs.

R. P. C. Hanson

A state of mind that sees God in everything is evidence of growth in grace and a thankful heart.

Charles G. Finney

Discover Your Passion

Do you have a fire burning deep within you—a desire for something more, something you cannot quite identify? Discovering what you are most passionate about—and then pursuing it— is essential if you want your life to rise above the level of lukewarm mediocrity.

Jesus said, "'Love the Lord your God with all your passion and prayer and intelligence.' This is the most important, the first on any list."
Matthew 22:37–38 MSG

T hink about the people who have made a difference in the world, in your community, in your personal life. Chances are good that the people who come to mind are those whose lives were driven by a passion that nothing could quench. Mother Teresa, who had an impact on countless people and inspired others to lives of service; a local leader whose tireless advocacy for the elderly led to improved conditions at the area senior center; or maybe your own mother, whose passion for her family helped make you the person you are today.

Now think about yourself. Have you discovered an overriding passion in your own life? Have you found the one thing that stirs your emotions and often consumes your thoughts? Maybe your

When you discover your mission, you will feel its demand. It will fill you with enthusiasm and a burning desire to get to work on it.
W. Clement Stone

passion is a career you have long believed you would be good at, a hobby you have always wanted to try, or a talent you have neglected for much too long. Second only to your passion for the things of God, this one pursuit lingers in the back of your mind and leaves you feeling discontented and unfulfilled.

It is time to stoke that fire within, regardless of your age or your circumstances. If you are like many people, you have just come up with a list of reasons why you don't even want to fan the embers: it is too late to create something meaningful from your life, you do not have the money you would need to pursue your interest, you will not be good at it once you try it, or your friends and family will try to discourage you. In short, you do not want to be disappointed—again.

Faith is the highest passion in a human being. Many in every generation may not come that far, but none comes further.
— Søren Kierkegaard

Maybe you think pursuing your passion involves changing your life in one great, dramatic gesture, and you are understandably afraid to make such a commitment. You can overcome that fear by simply taking one small step. Instead of enrolling in a full-time master's program, take an online course that will bring you a bit closer to that career goal. If you have always wanted to try your hand at painting, you do not need to equip a full artist's studio; grab a brush and some paint, and express yourself with abandon. Did you give up your love of the theater once you graduated from college? Or can you audition for a small part in a community production?

The world is full of people whose "first steps" resulted in life-changing pursuits. The ones who grab the headlines are the celebrities—the destitute garage band that followed their dream and ended up with a multimillion-dollar recording contract. But pursuing your passion does not always result in a grandiose outcome; you may be more like the successful attorney who gave up a potential six-figure salary early in his career to do what he really loved, working on Harley-Davidsons. His reward was sheer joy and contentment, even though it meant downsizing, cutting back, and living on an uncertain income.

The important thing is that you understand the effect this could have on your entire future. Discovering and pursuing your passion offers you an opportunity for a richly rewarding life. Given the choice, would you prefer to continue in the direction you are now going or blaze a new path?

You have that choice. Make the decision today to stop ignoring the passion that is lying

interesting to note

The National Institute of Mental Health reported that the amount of dopamine, the "pleasure" chemical found in the brain, declines with age. To offset this loss, mental health professionals tell aging patients to begin enjoying activities they found fulfilling when they were younger. For many, that means pursuing their passion.

Will you put up with a little foolish aside from me? Please, just for a moment. The thing that has me so upset is that I care about you so much—this is the passion of God burning inside me!

2 Corinthians 11:1–2 MSG

dormant within you. Not only will this impact your own life; your enthusiasm will also spill over into the lives of others, including your immediate family. Passion is infectious. As long as your pursuit does not become all-consuming—which is a potential side effect of passion—your love for what you are doing cannot help but have a positive effect on those around you.

what's essential

Spend some time reflecting on what energizes you and ignites your enthusiasm. What is holding you back from engaging in that activity? What is preventing you from taking that first small step? Give all your fears and objections to God, and trust him for any resources you think you may need.

DO pursue whatever it is in life that you are most passionate about.

DO encourage others to discover the origin of the fire that burns within them.

DON'T allow negative people to stifle your interest and enthusiasm.

DON'T let your passion cross the line to become an obsession.

Find Contentment

A wise man—the apostle Paul—once wrote, "I have learned how to be content with whatever I have" (Philippians 4:11 NLT). Contentment, it seems, does not come naturally to everyone. It is a quality that must be cultivated and maintained. But how do you find contentment in a society that encourages you to want more?

W hen you are content, you are satisfied with what you own, how you live, and whatever else defines your life—your job, your family, your church, and so forth. For many people who would describe themselves as "content," that satisfaction came after a long struggle with the desire for something more or at least something different.

But is that desire wrong? Without discontentment, how could you improve your lot in life? What would motivate you to contribute to making the world a better place? And why would you make an effort to grow spiritually?

To answer those and other questions, it is important to understand what contentment is and what it isn't—starting with the latter.

> Godliness with contentment is great gain. For we brought nothing into the world, and we can take nothing out of it. But if we have food and clothing, we will be content with that.
>
> 1 Timothy 6:6–8 NIV

> Being content with an attic ought not to mean being unable to move from it and resigned to living in it; it ought to mean appreciating all there is in such a position.
>
> G. K. Chesterton

What contentment is not. Contentment is not resignation. A contented person is not a defeated person. True contentment never asks, "Why bother? What is the point?" Neither does true contentment equal an excuse for inaction. John Graham, a nineteenth-century meatpacker, once wrote, "There are two kinds of discontent in this world: the discontent that works, and the discontent that wrings its hands." The "discontent that works" is compatible with contentment; the key is in finding satisfaction in your efforts to make things better, without fretting, without worrying, without complaining.

 It is not our circumstances that create our discontent or contentment. It is us.
— Vivian Greene

What contentment is. Contentment doesn't wring its hands; it wrings every bit of good out of every situation. Contentment recognizes and accepts each situation for what it is and realizes that there is something to be gained from every experience in life. Contented people are grateful for their possessions, no matter how few they may be. They see clearly what others do not, that contentment comes from within.

Faith-based contentment acknowledges that true contentment accompanies a life devoted to God. If you love God "with all your heart and with all your soul and with all your strength" (Deuteronomy 6:5 NIV), there is little room in your life for discontentment. If you believe God "will generously provide all you need" (2 Corinthians 9:8 NLT), you are confident that you have enough—in fact, more than enough. And if you acknowledge the wisdom of Jesus, you understand that contentment is crucial to your spiritual growth, because he taught that "the lure of wealth and the desire for other things" (Mark 4:19 NLT) can choke the life out of your relationship with God.

Finding contentment in an environment that promotes "the desire for other things" may seem challenging, but you can begin to be content by following a few simple steps:

- Acknowledge God's current provision and trust him for your future needs. God will never leave you (Hebrews 13:5), and he will give you whatever you need (Matthew 6:25–32).

- Realize that everything in this world is transitory. You brought nothing into the world, and you will take nothing out with you (1 Timothy 6:7).

- Recognize what is truly essential to sustain life. Paul narrows that down to food and clothing (1 Timothy 6:8), but it is not unreasonable to add such things as shelter, transportation, and an income. The important thing is to be aware of how little you need to be content.

- Understand that material possessions never bring long-lasting satisfaction. "Whoever loves money never has money enough; whoever loves wealth is never satisfied with his income," according to Ecclesiastes 5:10 (NIV).

interesting to note

Philosopher Johann Wolfgang von Goethe narrowed contentment down to nine factors: (1) health to work, (2) strength to overcome, (3) grace to live right, (4) patience to do good, (5) charity to befriend neighbors, (6) love to be useful, (7) hope to remove fear, (8) wealth to meet needs, and (9) faith to "make real the things of God."

I know how to live on almost nothing or with everything. I have learned the secret of living in every situation, whether it is with a full stomach or empty, with plenty or little.

Philippians 4:12 NLT

Too many people make the mistake of thinking that if they just had a few more things—a bigger house, maybe, or a certain position at work—they would be content. That is a false assumption. Contentment begins right now, in your current situation—a situation that a loving God is well aware of.

what's essential

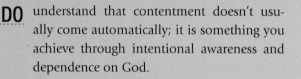

First Timothy 6:6 speaks not just of contentment but also of godliness. It is essential that your contentment be accompanied by a commitment to godly living—which in turn results in even greater contentment. That is the "great gain" Paul wrote to Timothy about (6:6 NIV).

DO understand that contentment doesn't usually come automatically; it is something you achieve through intentional awareness and dependence on God.

DO express gratitude for what you have and thank God that he has provided for all your needs.

DON'T confuse contentment with resignation; contentment is no excuse for refusing to take action when it is needed.

DON'T allow the desire for "more" to interfere with your relationship with God.

Maintain Your Integrity

There's a well-known story of a wealthy rancher who suddenly lost his ten children, his possessions, his servants, and his livelihood, more than eleven thousand head of livestock. But even after suffering this great loss, Job would continue to be known as a man of integrity—for thousands of years to come.

The Bible describes Job as "the finest man in all the earth . . . a man of complete integrity" (Job 1:8 NLT). He revered God. He avoided evil. He regularly offered sacrifices in case his sons or daughters had committed some unknown sin. And yet, when he lost nearly everything, he never blamed God. In fact, he praised him (Job 1:22).

But when Job broke out in horrible boils from head to foot, his wife—the sole surviving member of his family—had had enough of his integrity. She told him he should "curse God and die" (Job 2:9 NLT). He refused to utter one word against God. And though he later questioned and challenged God, at the end of the story, Job's integrity remained intact.

Job's integrity did not come naturally to him, and it doesn't come naturally to anyone else. It takes intentional effort, determination, and dependence on God to become a person of integrity. It takes deciding ahead of time that your behavior will remain consistent with your beliefs and values. It takes, as it has been said, making a commitment to always do the right thing—even when no one is looking.

 If humanity does not opt for integrity we are through completely. It is absolutely touch and go. Each one of us could make the difference.
—Buckminster Fuller

How do you know if you truly have this quality? If you are a person of integrity,

- you refuse to compromise your principles. You adhere to a set of nonnegotiable convictions;

- you cannot be bought. No amount of money would entice you to do something unethical;

- you resist negative cultural influences. You maintain a standard of excellence in your behavior even as society around you sinks into mediocrity;

- you make decisions based on what is right. It may be expedient to do otherwise, but your conscience will always choose the honorable over the convenient;

- you place a high priority on honesty. You do not just tell the truth; you also look at yourself with a clear eye and live an authentic life that is true to who you are;

- you treat others with dignity, courtesy, and respect. You believe your behavior toward others is a reflection of character;

- you defend your convictions, regardless of the cost. Others may remain noncommittal, but you stand up for what you believe to be right, no matter how unpopular that stance may be.

Does all that mean you are perfect? No. But it does mean you are honorable, trustworthy, responsible, incorruptible, disciplined, and relentlessly committed to doing the right thing. "We struggle daily with situations that demand decisions between what we want to do and what we ought to do," John Maxwell said. "Integrity establishes the ground rules for resolving these tensions. It determines who we are and how we will respond before the conflict even appears. Integrity welds what we say, think, and do into a whole person so that permission is never granted for one of these to be out of sync."

Becoming that "whole person" is an essential part of your life with God—and every area of your life. Having integrity means doing what is right in both the little and the big things at your job, at your church, in your community, in your family—even on the road. Maybe you wouldn't manipulate the sales figures at work, but you've been known to cut off a driver or two when you are in a rush. If that behavior isn't compatible with your values, that is an area to work on.

interesting to note

The word *integrity* stems from a Latin word that means "entire" or "complete." The character of a person of integrity is fully integrated rather than fractured by contradiction. In addition to "honesty" and "wholeness," *honor* is a synonym for *integrity*; a person of integrity is a person of honor.

You yourself must be an example to them by doing good works of every kind. Let everything you do reflect the integrity and seriousness of your teaching.

Titus 2:7 NLT

It is unlikely that you will experience the measure of loss and suffering that Job did. But can you maintain your integrity regardless of what you may face? Decide now that you can and will—and live in accordance with that decision.

what's essential

If you are a person of integrity, you live a life of fearless transparency. You have no ulterior motives, no clandestine agenda, and no secret schemes that are hidden from others. On the contrary, you welcome accountability—because you know your life can withstand the close scrutiny of God and other people.

DO decide ahead of time that you will always do what you believe is right no matter the consequences; that will help simplify many of your future decisions.

DO understand that you cannot claim to have "some" integrity; you either have it or you don't.

DON'T think that integrity will become a part of your nature without effort; integrity results from deliberate commitment and action.

DON'T "fracture" your life and your character by trying to maintain integrity at church but not at work, in your community but not at home.

Hold On to Hope

For people of faith, hope is inseparable from God. Too often, though, even people of faith confuse "hope" with "hopes"—their wishes and dreams that something specific will happen. But authentic hope is rooted in the assurance that no matter what the outcome, God will see you through.

Hope does not disappoint, because the love of God has been poured out in our hearts by the Holy Spirit who was given to us.

Romans 5:5 NKJV

When a shoulder injury forced tennis star Andrea Jaeger to retire from competition at the age of nineteen, fans of the sport wondered what would become of her. She was the first female tennis player to turn pro at fourteen, and until she was injured, tennis had seemingly been her life.

But away from the cameras and the microphones, Andrea had a growing relationship with God and a heart for terminally ill children. Instead of dwelling on her injury, she considered her early retirement to be a blessing, because it meant she could finally serve God full-time.

Andrea parlayed her tennis winnings and her knack for fund-raising into a camp for children with cancer, many of them terminally ill. For decades now, she has said good-bye to far too many

As long as there is one upright man, as long as there is one compassionate woman, the contagion may spread and the scene is not desolate. Hope is the thing left to us in a bad time.

E. B. White

campers who lost their lives at a very young age. And yet, Andrea's life and work continue to exist on a rock-solid foundation of hope.

How can Andrea and her staff remain hopeful in the face of a disease that ravages so many lives? How can they go on when they know full well that the campers they give their time and effort and love to this year may not be alive next year? Andrea will be the first to tell you that the hope they cling to so tenaciously is one that has little to do with an expected outcome.

Hope is not the conviction that something will turn out well, but the certainty that something makes sense regardless of how it turns out.
— Václav Havel

What that means is that while Andrea would love to see every child restored to perfect health, she knows this will not happen. Her hope rests on the goodness and faithfulness of God, the one who will see the children and their families, as well as Andrea and her staff, through every ordeal, every death, and every sorrow that comes their way.

Andrea's hope may be tested to a greater extent than that of others, but the measure of her hope is available to everyone—including you. You can activate that hope by forgetting about a specific outcome altogether and instead believing that regardless of the outcome, you will endure and maybe even make sense of the situation someday. It also helps to consider the alternatives. If you hope for particular results, you will undoubtedly face disappointments; if you lose hope completely, you will become cynical, bitter, and totally miserable. As Dr. Bernie Siegel once pointed out, "In the face of uncertainty, there is nothing wrong with hope." Those are words worth remembering.

Be forewarned, though. Not everyone shares that hope, and some people will undermine your optimism by saying you are naive or deluded or a victim of wishful thinking. And they may come close to convincing you of that, especially if your circumstances appear hopeless to your detractors. This is when you need to develop both a steely resolve and a stockpile of gracious responses. Begin to think of your hope as untouchable, so that even the most vocal naysayers cannot penetrate the wall that protects it. And as for those gracious responses, that is biblical; 1 Peter 3:15 says you should "always be prepared to give an answer to everyone who asks you to give the reason for the hope that you have. But do this with gentleness and respect" (NIV).

Author Gerald May discovered an intimate connection between God and hope when he visited Bosnia during the war that made "ethnic cleansing" a household phrase. There he met people whose expressions conveyed an inexplicable ray of hope, despite the loss of everything they held dear—including many of their loved ones. May began questioning them; were they hoping for peace, for help from the United Nations, for U.S. intervention? They answered no to every question. How, then, could they have hope, if there was nothing to hope for? Their answer? *Bog,* the Serbo-Croatian word for God.

Why are you cast down, O my soul? And why are you disquieted within me? Hope in God, for I shall yet praise Him for the help of His countenance.
Psalm 42:5 NKJV

That, in the end, is the answer to the hope that lies within you. When God is your hope, the outcome of every situation takes on meaning and purpose. You may not understand what that is, but God has seen you through for a reason. He was with you every step of the way, strengthening you, encouraging you, and helping you to endure. And you can safely cling to the hope that he will do the same in the future—no matter what.

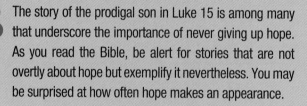

what's essential

 The story of the prodigal son in Luke 15 is among many that underscore the importance of never giving up hope. As you read the Bible, be alert for stories that are not overtly about hope but exemplify it nevertheless. You may be surprised at how often hope makes an appearance.

DO remember that hope does not depend on specific outcomes.

DO ask God to restore your hope as soon as you begin to feel as if you are losing hope.

DON'T give up by letting go of the hope that lies within you, however small you think it may be.

DON'T ever think of hope as something as simplistic as wishful thinking.

Have Compassion for Others

While the literal meaning of compassion is "suffering with," down through the centuries the Christian understanding of the word has also included the idea of helping to alleviate suffering. By that definition, a truly compassionate person becomes immersed in the suffering of others and does whatever possible to ease their pain. And there is no better example of compassionate living than the life of Jesus.

During his three-year ministry on earth, Jesus modeled *compassion*, the word used to describe his motivation for feeding the masses and healing the sick. His actions and words not only showed his deep love and concern for people in need; they also conveyed the power to heal people of their physical disorders and illnesses, meet their needs, transform their spiritual lives, and restore them to wholeness

That model, though, can become intimidating if you apply it too literally to your own life. Having compassion on others—sharing their suffering

If someone has enough money to live well and sees a brother or sister in need but shows no compassion—how can God's love be in that person?

1 John 3:17 NLT

The value of compassion cannot be overemphasized. Anyone can criticize. It takes a true believer to be compassionate. No greater burden can be borne by an individual than to know no one cares or understands.

Arthur H. Stainback

and doing what you can to alleviate it—doesn't mean duplicating Jesus' ministry of healing, transformation, and restoration. It means sensing the deep need of others, empathizing with them, and asking God to show you how you can be of help to them, with your own set of gifts, talents, skills, and resources. Your compassion lives at the intersection of faith and action, believing God can use you to comfort others and ease their distress in a tangible way.

Man may dismiss compassion from his heart, but God never will.
—William Cowper

James 2:15–16 offers a challenge to those whose compassion exists only on an empathetic level: "If a brother or sister is without clothing and in need of daily food, and one of you says to them, 'Go in peace, be warmed and be filled,' and yet you do not give them what is necessary for their body, what use is that?" (NASB). The benediction—"Go in peace, be warmed and be filled"—indicates that the one speaking acknowledges the need for clothing and food and hopes that the need will be met. That is not true compassion; compassionate people do what they can to meet the needs of others, even if it means sacrificing their own comfort.

How can you show compassion to others? Some ways are obvious, such as giving a financial gift or needed items to a homeless shelter, soup kitchen, or other ministry to the poor. That is important, and many of those ministries and services could not exist without that kind of support. But that is also an impersonal means of showing compassion. Showing compassion on a more personal level can get downright uncomfortable—but the rewards more than compensate for your discomfort.

Compassion gets more personal when you volunteer with a group that ministers to people in need, whether they are homeless, impoverished, terminally ill, jobless, abused, or anything else. But people in need are all around you; you do not have to look far to find people who need to know that you care on a deep level. In many ways, it is easier to show compassion to the homeless than to show compassion to your neighbor, your coworker, or even a family member. But God doesn't ask you to do difficult things without giving you the ability to accomplish them.

Is your neighbor going through a painful divorce? Has one of your coworkers lost a loved one? Is someone in your church facing eviction? And what about all those acquaintances who are clearly hurting but are ashamed to let you know why? Letting them know you care, by listening, offering practical help, and promising confidentiality can help immensely in the short run. But letting them know you will be there for them in the long run—walking alongside them, sharing in their pain, offering a shoulder, a hug, a meal, a prayer—can change their lives.

interesting to note

Small acts of compassion can have a powerful effect in the workplace, according to University of Michigan researchers. They discovered that such acts as "lending an ear, extending a hand, or being present to someone in pain" helped shape long-lasting, positive attitudes and behaviors among employees.

He arose and came to his father. But when he was still a great way off, his father saw him and had compassion, and ran and fell on his neck and kissed him.

Luke 15:20 NKJV

Obviously, you cannot become immersed in the suffering of every needy person you meet. But showing compassion by doing what you can for even one person might make all the difference in the life of that one person—and that is no small accomplishment.

what's essential

The eleventh edition of Merriam-Webster's Collegiate Dictionary defines compassion as "sympathetic consciousness of others' distress together with a desire to alleviate it." Compassion turns that desire into action. Compassion involves getting involved, even if it means getting your hands dirty and taking risks.

DO be sensitive to the need around you and ask God how he can use you to help meet that need.

DO be prepared for God to lead you to some unexpected places where you will find people you never thought you'd describe as "needy."

DON'T confuse sympathy with compassion; sympathy is an emotional response to a sad situation, but compassion becomes immersed in the suffering of the people involved.

DON'T substitute impersonal acts of compassion for one-on-one involvement; both are important, but personal acts of compassion are crucial.

What Should My Character Reflect?

LOVE

Let all those rejoice who put their trust in You; let them ever shout for joy, because You defend them; let those also who love Your name be joyful in You. For You, O LORD, will bless the righteous; with favor You will surround him as with a shield.

Psalm 5:11–12 NKJV

The day will come when, after harnessing the winds, the tides and gravitation, we shall harness for God the energies of Love. And on that day, for the second time in the history of the world, man will have discovered fire.

Teilhard de Chardin

Love is what is left in a relationship after all the selfishness is taken out.

Nick Richardson

Capture the Joy of Living

God, the Creator of the universe, loves you so much that nothing can ever separate you from that love. What is more, he promises to be with you every day and see you through every situation you will face for the rest of your life. What's not to be joyful about?

You'll go out in joy, you'll be led into a whole and complete life. The mountains and hills will lead the parade, bursting with song. All the trees of the forest will join the procession, exuberant with applause.

Isaiah 55:12 MSG

To those who have never experienced it in its purest form, joy is among the most misunderstood of all human emotions. Some equate joy with happiness that is tied to an experience, perhaps, or a relationship, or maybe even an ongoing situation they find themselves in. As long as that experience, relationship, or situation remains a pleasant one, they may believe that they've encountered the real thing: joy.

Be merry, really merry. The life of a true Christian should be a perpetual jubilee, a prelude to the festivals of eternity.

Theophane Venard

But what happens when things turn unpleasant, when troubles come and life begins to fall apart? What happens when it becomes impossible to find any happiness in your circumstances? If you have mistakenly tied joy to feelings of happiness, what you thought was joy will evaporate in no time.

One of the keys to capturing the joy of living is to separate joy from happiness. Happiness depends on favorable circumstances; joy survives and even thrives in unfavorable circumstances. Some have gone so far as to call joy the opposite of happiness; happiness is superficial and fleeting, they maintain, while joy is profound and eternal, rooted in a deep and abiding sense of the presence of God.

Real joy comes not from ease or riches or from the praise of men, but from doing something worthwhile.
—Pierre Corneille

Experiencing pure joy in the midst of difficulties is a hallmark of a life devoted to God. The New Testament is replete with references to joy amid challenges, such as the account of Paul and Silas praying and singing while they were chained up in prison (Acts 16:25). The following verses are among those that underscore the presence of joy amid trials:

- "We can rejoice, too, when we run into problems and trials, for we know that they help us develop endurance" (Romans 5:3 NLT).

- "Out of the most severe trial, their [the Macedonians'] overflowing joy and their extreme poverty welled up in rich generosity" (2 Corinthians 8:2 NIV).

- "Dear brothers and sisters, when troubles come your way, consider it an opportunity for great joy" (James 1:2 NLT).

- "In this you greatly rejoice, even though now for a little while, if necessary, you have been distressed by various trials" (1 Peter 1:6 NASB).

- "Rejoice that you participate in the sufferings of Christ, so that you may be overjoyed when his glory is revealed" (1 Peter 4:13 NIV).

Another key to experiencing joy is understanding that joy is inseparable from gratitude. A person who is grateful to God for all of life is a joyful person. Author Lewis Smedes discovered this for himself following a stirring concert by Isaac Stern. As Stern gratefully and joyfully acknowledged the thundering applause, Smedes saw an illustration of joy. In response to the blessing and joy of receiving an extraordinary gift (Stern's talent), the people expressed their gratitude by returning the blessing (a resounding standing ovation).

This came to illustrate Smedes's life with God. God gave him the gift of life, and out of gratitude he wanted to bless God in return. "Joy is an intermezzo of gratitude that interrupts the routine motion of life," Smedes wrote. "There comes a sense that life—now, here, today—is a gift worth blessing God for. When it comes, when this sense of being a gift comes, joy has come to us."

Has joy come to you? Do you see your life as a gift worth blessing God for—worth thanking God for? Have you traded in the need for the fleeting pleasure of happiness in favor of an eternal joy that thrives regardless of the circumstances? That joy is yours for the taking when you see all of life as a gift from God—and bless him in return with your gratitude.

what's essential

Jesus emphasized the love of God so that his followers would be filled with joy (John 15:11). The early Christians found great joy in their lives together (Acts 2:46). Paul encouraged Christians to rejoice (Romans 12:15; Philippians 4:4). Joy goes hand in hand with the Christian life.

DO express your gratitude to God for the life he has given you; a life overflowing with gratitude is a joyful life.

DO recognize that you can experience genuine joy in the midst of life's greatest challenges.

DON'T confuse happiness with joy; happiness depends on favorable circumstances, while joy can flourish under all circumstances.

DON'T forget that nothing can separate you from God's love, which alone is reason enough to be joyful.

Extend Grace to Everyone

One of the clearest of Jesus' instructions to his followers was this one: "Freely you have received, freely give" (Matthew 10:8 NKJV). In context, he was speaking of spiritual gifts. One of the spiritual gifts God has freely given to you is grace—his unmerited favor and undeserved kindness. It is a gift he wants you to freely give to others.

You probably do not find it difficult to extend kindness and goodwill to people who have treated you likewise. But what about the people in your life—and you know who they are—who deserve nothing less than your contempt? Few people get through life without being wronged, betrayed, abandoned, or abused in some way by others who show no remorse for their actions. How can God expect you to grant those people any consideration at all?

Easily—and with great difficulty. Easily, because God has set an example for you. He freely bestowed his grace on you when you turned your heart toward him. You hadn't done a thing to earn his grace, his favor on your life. But he gave it to

Many Christians seem to understand the concept of being saved by grace, but they have missed the concept of being sustained by grace.

James D. Mallory Jr.

you anyway, because of the depth of his love for you. And with great difficulty, because you are not God, and God is well aware of that. But even as every bit of your humanity resists extending grace to the undeserving, God gives you the spiritual fortitude to fight your base instincts, draw on God's power to do what is right, and lavish grace on those who have wronged you.

Sound impossible? It isn't, and it gets easier with time. That is because the first time you extend grace to another person, you may experience a joy the likes of which you have never known before. Not only will the experience serve as a vivid reminder of the grace God granted, and continues to grant, to you; it will also demonstrate the fact that you can have victory over those base instincts that so often trip you up.

 Grace is the very opposite of merit . . . Grace is not only undeserved favor, but it is favor shown to the one who has deserved the very opposite.
—Harry Ironside

The grace of God was so important to the apostle Paul that every letter attributed to him begins and ends with a message pertaining to grace. In several of his letters, he instructed the heirs of grace—those who have received the inheritance of God's grace as his children—on how they should behave toward one another, frequently using the word *gracious.* He instructed the church at Corinth to graciously forgive a repentant person whose wrongdoing had caused great pain (2 Corinthians 2:7). In several places, he described his work and that of the church as "gracious" (2 Corinthians 8:6,19 NASB). He urged the followers of Christ to focus their thoughts on that which is gracious (Philippians 4:8), speak words that are filled with grace (Colossians 4:6), and graciously practice hospitality, even to strangers (1 Peter 4:9).

How do you become that gracious? To missionary E. Stanley Jones, extending grace to others is an outgrowth of your relationship to the ultimate Giver of grace: "Grace binds you with far stronger cords than the cords of duty or obligation can bind you. Grace is free, but when once you take it, you are bound forever to the Giver and bound to catch the spirit of the Giver. Like produces like. Grace makes you gracious, the Giver makes you give."

Maybe you do not think you are ready to extend grace to a sibling who humiliated you at a recent holiday gathering—and every holiday gathering for as long as you can remember. For now, try responding graciously in a less painful situation—say, when the dry cleaner ruins one of your suits. Work your way up to granting grace to a colleague who took credit for one of your ideas.

Finally, shove the resentment, the hurt, and the bad memories aside. Trust God to give you the strength to treat other people with the undeserved gift of grace. You may be more ready than you thought.

what's essential

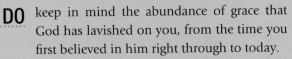

There's an unlimited supply of grace to be received from God and to be given away. It is unlikely that you will ever run out of opportunities to pass it along. Be sensitive to God's leading as you encounter people who could use a dose of the grace you have in abundance.

DO extend grace freely to the people in your life who do not deserve it and would never expect it.

DO keep in mind the abundance of grace that God has lavished on you, from the time you first believed in him right through to today.

DON'T allow opportunities to extend grace to others pass you by, robbing you of the joy that comes with obeying God and treating others kindly.

DON'T ignore Paul's admonitions regarding gracious behavior, such as focusing your thoughts and your words on that which is grace-filled.

Show Your Appreciation

Appreciation, gratitude, thankfulness—all describe a response to a gift, a favor, or some kind of help. For many people, the emotion is a natural one; who wouldn't feel thankful for something beneficial to them? But some of those same people often forget the next step—expressing their gratitude.

Can you see the holiness in those things you take for granted—a paved road or a washing machine? If you concentrate on finding what is good in every situation, you will discover that your life will suddenly be filled with gratitude, a feeling that nurtures the soul.

Harold Kushner

When you give someone a gift and he dismisses it without acknowledgment, you tend to notice. You also tend to notice when the recipient goes the extra mile to reach you personally and tell you how much your kind gesture meant to him. Quite the contrast, isn't it?

Appreciation, gratitude, and thankfulness are meant to be expressed. When they are not, you cannot help but wonder what is going on, even if you are not offended by the oversight. Did the recipient not like the gift, not appreciate the favor, not welcome the help? Holocaust survivor Elie Wiesel said there is something wrong with such a person: "When a person doesn't have gratitude, something is missing in his or her humanity. A person can almost be defined by his or her attitude toward gratitude."

How does your attitude toward gratitude define you? Think about how you respond the moment you receive something for which you are genuinely grateful—maybe an offer to babysit for a weekend so you and your spouse can have some time alone. Very likely, your first split-second response is a very private one. *How did she know I wanted that—needed that? I never told anyone!* But just as quickly as those thoughts come and go, another one surfaces. *Thank you! Thank you!* Imagine keeping that to yourself. You couldn't, could you? You would have to express your gratitude. Even if you couldn't actually get the words out, you'd find a way to show your appreciation. Deep gratitude may take root on the inside, but it usually cannot help but reveal itself on the outside.

As we express our gratitude, we must never forget that the highest appreciation is not to utter words, but to live by them.
— John F. Kennedy

And yet, people who are generous with their gratitude for the big things sometimes overlook the need to show appreciation for the seemingly small things—a teenage son's attempts to remember to fill the gas tank after he has used a parent's car, the cleaning crew's efforts to make the office bathroom sparkle, the landscape team's ongoing struggle to keep the church property weed-free. They may seem small, but those are important and often thankless tasks.

interesting to note

A study conducted by sociologist Robert Emmons determined that grateful people are happier and healthier; are less inclined to be angry, depressed, or stressed out; exercise more; experience less pain; offer more emotional support to others; sleep better; have a positive outlook on life; and tend to fulfill their goals.

They refreshed my spirit and yours. Therefore acknowledge such men.
1 Corinthians 16:18 NKJV

Likewise, thanking God for the big things—the birth or adoption of a much-wanted baby or an anonymous monetary gift that arrived just in time to keep the utilities on—may come easily. But again, the seemingly small things often go unacknowledged until the situation changes. The peace and quiet you've enjoyed for years is shattered when a noisy neighbor moves in. The car that never gave you a problem fails to start when you are running late to catch a flight. The stray cat that took up residence in your yard has moved on—and the mice have moved in.

All of a sudden, you realize you were never grateful to God for all those little things. Instead, you took them for granted. This would be a good time to start thanking God for your new neighbor, the faulty starter, and even the mice; cultivating a grateful attitude will almost certainly change your perspective and may even change the situation.

Look around you. Take notice of all the things you have to be grateful for. Take your eyes off what is missing—the things you want but cannot have—and focus on what is present. You very likely have so much more than you lack. Be thankful for everything; even misfortune can contain hidden blessings. Find the good in every aspect of your life. Thank the people who have made so much of the good in your life possible. Thank God for bringing those people into your life. And thank God for life itself—all of life, the good and the bad, the big and the little, and everything in between.

what's essential

Gratefulness is not a denial of the bad in the world or the difficulties in your life. It simply tips the scales in favor of the good by keeping the focus on the many blessings in life. A grateful heart acknowledges pain while giving thanks for efforts to alleviate it.

DO give voice to your gratitude; let others know how thankful you are for both the big and the little things in your life.

DO focus on all that you have been given rather than all that you think you need.

DON'T try to pretend that bad things do not happen; denying difficulties only creates more problems.

DON'T ignore the physical, emotional, mental, and spiritual benefits of cultivating a thankful attitude toward life.

Open Up Your Heart

In the 2002 film Unconditional Love, *scorned wife Grace Beasley concludes that love does indeed come with conditions attached to it. For her, having unconditional love for her husband is impossible. Well, of course it is. She's trying to love him without the help of God, the Creator of unconditional love.*

In all the literature about love in the English language, one passage in the Bible is considered to be equal in literary value to the works of Shakespeare, Lord Byron, Elizabeth Barrett Browning, and other classical poets who wrote about love. That passage is 1 Corinthians 13. In fewer than three hundred words, the apostle Paul gave a beautiful, eloquent description of love, one that two millennia later continues to be lauded by scholars, cherished by Christians, and quoted in both religious and secular wedding ceremonies.

But for all its literary magnificence, 1 Corinthians 13 has some difficult things to say about love. The words may lift the spirits of the happy couple on their big day, but living them out in the everydayness of the marriage to follow is another matter altogether. In fact, Paul's words are so crucial to the couple's future that they would have been better off studying it in premarital counseling than being captivated by it during the ceremony.

You will find, as you look back upon your life, that the moments when you really lived are the moments when you have done things in the spirit of love.
— Henry Drummond

Look at what one portion of the chapter really says about genuine love and consider what that looks like in your own life—whether or not you are married. Though the 1 Corinthians 13 has been adopted for use in weddings, nowhere does Paul limit his definition to romantic love; the principles apply to all relationships:

- *Love suffers long and is kind (v. 4 NKJV)*. Are you patient with your spouse, with others? Are you able to let go of minor irritations and deal with major ones calmly, without being unkind? Do you treat your family and close friends with as much kindness as you do the people you need to impress—your pastor, maybe, or the person who holds the key to your next promotion at work?

- *Love does not envy (v. 4 NKJV)*. A friend overtook you long ago on the road to prosperity; your spouse receives the applause and attention of her peers while you are virtually ignored. Can you honestly say you are not envious?

- *Love does not parade itself, is not puffed up (v. 4 NKJV)*. Maybe you are the spouse who receives all that applause and attention from your peers. Are you flaunting that, even just a little bit?

- *[Love] does not behave rudely, does not seek its own, is not provoked, thinks no evil (v. 5 NKJV).* Common courtesy. Selflessness. Graciously controlling negative feelings. Eliminating such things as suspicion and revenge from your thoughts. How's that working for you?

- *[Love] does not rejoice in iniquity, but rejoices in the truth (v. 6 NKJV).* Smugness—that feeling of self-satisfaction when someone gets caught in a lie or some other failing. Ever experience that? Or do you focus instead on the truth and rejoicing in it when you see evidence of truthfulness in the people you love?

- *[Love] bears all things, believes all things, hopes all things, endures all things (v. 7 NKJV).* Do you shoulder the burdens imposed on you by those you love? Do you believe the best about your spouse, your family, your friends? Do you exhibit optimism even amid strife and conflict with your loved ones? Can you survive difficult times without complaint or blaming others?

- *Love never fails (v. 8 NKJV).* Genuine love, the love God gives you to share with others, doesn't fail. Human love, the emotion that lacks a solid grounding in the love of God, can and does fail, all too often.

Paul's definition of genuine love may seem out of reach for humans, but it is the ideal that imperfect people are to strive for. Had the character of Grace Beasley opened her heart and allowed the biblical view of love to permeate her life, she could have caught a glimpse of unconditional love—right here on earth, right in her own marriage. Real people can too.

what's essential

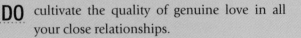

If you wanted to choose one character quality to work on, *agape* love would be a great candidate. *Agape* love encompasses all others. By its very nature, *agape*, which in Greek carries the connotation of self-sacrifice, purifies the love you have for your family, your friends—and your spouse.

DO cultivate the quality of genuine love in all your close relationships.

DO take the definitions of love in 1 Corinthians 13 seriously and allow them to become personal to you.

DON'T confuse the emotion of love, which can be fleeting, with the character quality of God's love, which is eternal.

DON'T think that your good works and charitable endeavors can be a substitute for sacrificially loving others.

Give Credit Where It Is Due

In late 2008, Miami banker Leonard Abess sold his stock in the bank he owned—and promptly distributed $60 million in proceeds among 471 current and former bank employees. Why? Abess said his employees were equally responsible for the bank's success, and he wanted to acknowledge that. That is giving credit where it is due—and cash as well.

Along with mismanagement, dishonesty, and greed, arrogance has been blamed for causing the economic collapse that brought down so many huge financial institutions in recent years. Arrogance and its close cousin, pride, are the opposite of humility. Arrogance lords over others and takes credit for every success, whether or not it is warranted. Humility stands aside, nudges others into the limelight, and acknowledges their contributions to every successful endeavor.

The Bible has a great deal to say about the way God rewards those who are humble—and penalizes those who are arrogant. Most people have heard that "pride goes before a fall," an adage based on

Always be humble and gentle. Be patient with each other, making allowance for each other's faults because of your love.

Ephesians 4:2 NLT

What makes humility so desirable is the marvelous thing it does to us; it creates in us a capacity for the closest possible intimacy with God.

Monica Baldwin

Proverbs 16:18. Had the financial executives, securities regulators, and elected officials—some arrogant, some humble—peered further into the Bible, they would have learned much more about God's perspective on pride and humility:

- "He leads the humble in what is right, and the humble He teaches His way" (Psalm 25:9 AMP).

- "The reward of humility and the fear of the LORD are riches, honor and life" (Proverbs 22:4 NASB).

- "Pride will ruin people, but those who are humble will be honored" (Proverbs 29:23 NCV).

 It is no great thing to be humble when you are brought low; but to be humble when you are praised is a great and rare attainment.
—Saint Bernard

- "Those who exalt themselves will be humbled, and those who humble themselves will be exalted" (Matthew 23:12 NLT).

- "Humble yourselves before the Lord, and he will lift you up" (James 4:10 NIV).

- "When pride comes, then comes shame; but with the humble is wisdom" (Proverbs 11:2 NKJV).

- "Fear-of-GOD is a school in skilled living—first you learn humility, then you experience glory" (Proverbs 15:33 MSG).

With all those promises, you'd think more people would aspire to be humble. But that is where irony comes in; a truly humble person did not become that way by seeking reward. Once you try

interesting to note

Young children often have a tender heart toward God. In Matthew 18:1–14, Jesus chose children as an example of the humility he wanted his disciples to exhibit. To those who wanted Jesus to seize political power, this would have made no sense. But few understood the honor God grants to the humble, then as now.

When you do things, do not let selfishness or pride be your guide. Instead, be humble and give more honor to others than to yourselves.

Philippians 2:3 NCV

to be humble in order to receive honor, you become proud. By contrast, humility reveals a grateful, loving, compassionate, and joyful heart, one that seeks the best for others.

Given that, it can be baffling when you encounter people who equate humility with weakness. Others associate it with humiliation—being shamed or embarrassed by someone—or humble in the sense of being insignificant or of low rank. Humility is actually a sign of courage, though once again, irony surfaces; a person of genuine humility would likely not think of himself as courageous.

It takes strength of character to be humble. The temptation to build yourself up is hard to resist in a culture so addicted to comparison. If you are not considered a success in the world's eyes, you may be tempted to make yourself seem successful; if you are considered a success, the temptation may be to make yourself look even better. And if you scoff at those who try to appear more successful than they are, you likely do so with a superior attitude—another sign of pride.

The surest way to develop the quality of humility is to submit yourself to God. When you strip yourself of your inflated sense of who you are, what you've accomplished, and what you can do for God; when you fall on your knees—or your face—in submission to God; when you stop telling God what you want and start listening to what he wants; when you begin to care more about God's opinion of you than other people's opinions of you, you are in a position to learn true humility.

You may never be in a position to give those around you the credit that is due them to the tune of $60 million. But you can start where you are, humbling yourself before God, moving to the sidelines, and showing the world what God and other people have done in your life.

what's essential

The next time you are tempted to build yourself up in the eyes of others, think about God's greatness and his many acts of kindness toward you. It is hard to take credit when the one who deserves all the credit is occupying your thoughts.

DO submit yourself to God and ask him to teach you true humility in the way you relate to other people.

DO remember to give God credit for all the good that has come your way.

DON'T compare yourself with others; comparison offers too many opportunities to succumb to pride.

DON'T confuse humility with humiliation or humbleness in the sense of low-ranking; humility is a virtue, not a weakness.

How Do I Live My Life Every Day?

WISDOM

The teachings of the LORD are perfect; they give new strength. The rules of the LORD can be trusted; they make plain people wise. The orders of the LORD are right; they make people happy. The commands of the LORD are pure; they light up the way.

Psalm 19:7–8 NCV

True wisdom, which will help us make our way through this complex world, begins by acknowledging the Lord and humbling ourselves before Him. It submits to the view that He knows best, and what this comes to us through . . . the special revelation of His Word.

Melvin Tinker

Knowledge comes by taking things apart. But wisdom comes by putting things together.

John A. Morrison

Decide What Matters Most

What do you think of when someone tells you that you have to prioritize your life? It is likely that you immediately imagine a list. For Christians, the list nearly always follows this sequence: (1) God; (2) family; (3) church; (4) work. But sometimes that just does not work. Well, what would happen if you threw away that list?

Seek (aim at and strive after) first of all His kingdom and His righteousness (His way of doing and being right), and then all these things taken together will be given you besides.

Matthew 6:33 AMP

One of the ironies in a Christian's life is inherent in the list above, which is so often taught as the way to order your priorities. That God is to take first place is a given; no one would argue with that. But the next three items can get muddled. You are barely making ends meet, and you need to take a part-time job that will help pay the bills but will also cut into family time. Your time commitment to church is starting to irritate your family, but you truly believe God has called you to serve the church as much as you do. You are employed by a company that requires you to work several Sundays a month, but your pastor gently reminds you that Sunday services should take precedence over work.

Do not have your concert first and tune your instruments afterward. Begin the day with God.

Hudson Taylor

And then there is everything else in your life, from whatever item 5 might be all the way through infinity. Volunteering, exercising, flossing, relaxing—all are important, but where do they fit on this imaginary list of priorities?

The things that matter the most in this world, they can never be held in our hand.
—Gloria Gaither

Relax. Nowhere in the Bible does God tell you to create a list of priorities. Throw away that list you've created in your head and start over—with this: "Seek first God's kingdom and what God wants. Then all your other needs will be met as well" (Matthew 6:33 NCV). There is your priority list. When you seek God first, everything else falls into place. Now you can begin to look at your life in a whole new way, something like the following— and in no particular order in terms of priority:

- *Seek God first for your family.* Trust God to help you make decisions that affect your family. If you have to work overtime, make arrangements for your family and trust God to take care of them in your absence. If God leads you to decline overtime or a second job, trust God to provide for your needs.

- *Seek God first at your church.* Seek God's clear direction on how and when you should serve your church, and how much time you are realistically able to serve. It may be more time than you are serving now, but it could also be less. It is sometimes difficult to say no to those who think you should give more of your time, but your responsibility is to seek God's will and listen to what he has to say.

- *Seek God first at work.* It is especially important to seek God for your work, because you may not be able to appeal to your boss on a spiritual level the way you can your family or church leadership. Working long hours, working on weekends, working at the whims of your boss can spell the difference between a paycheck and unemployment benefits. Trusting God may not mean defying your boss; it may mean trusting God that for now, it is all right to work long hours, weekends, and at your boss's discretion. Give God priority, and things will fall into place.

- *Seek God first at play.* Whether you are planning a major vacation or rounding up the family for a spontaneous trip to the beach, by seeking God first you have a better shot at enjoying a relaxing, fun time.

See how much easier that is than worrying over where everything should fit on a nice, neat list? Life isn't always nice and neat, and trying to prioritize a sometimes messy life according to a strict list adds to the stress.

interesting to note

The word *priority* entered the English language in the fourteenth century, but it was not until four hundred years later that *prior* as an adjective came into use (though it had long been used as a monastic title). And *prioritize*? English-speaking people did not start to *prioritize* until sometime during the 1972 presidential election.

What do you benefit if you gain the whole world but lose your own soul? Is anything worth more than your soul?
Mark 8:36–37 NLT

The components of your life will fluctuate with regard to the time and attention you give them, sometimes within the course of a single day. Keep God as your top priority, and let everything else fall into place—under his care.

what's essential

Trying to prioritize can complicate things rather than clarify them. If you have a priority list that works for you—and God has first place—by all means, keep it going! If not, remember Matthew 6:33. Memorize it, and keep its message close at hand. Seeking God— that's your first priority. And it could be your only one.

DO seek first the kingdom of God and believe that then all your other needs will be met.

DO realize that your life is unique, and God deals with you in unique ways.

DON'T expect a rigid list of priorities to work in every situation, at every point in your life.

DON'T allow others to dictate what your priorities should be; keep God first, and go to him to determine what is next in importance at this time, on this occasion, in this situation.

Simplify Your Lifestyle

Life can be so complicated. Some people seem to thrive on limitless activity, but many others yearn for a simpler life. Where, though, can anyone find that in a twenty-four/seven society? Conventional thinking is that it is just not possible. But try unconventional thinking for a change. Believe that a simpler life is possible—because in reality, it is.

It is a line heard in many a TV show and movie. The bad or troubled or distraught character is about to do something foolish or violent or tragic. The good or sane or kindhearted character is trying to stop the other character from doing whatever that something is. The next line is so predictable that you can say it before it is spoken: *It doesn't have to be this way.*

That's a great line to keep in mind when life threatens to overwhelm you with its exasperating details. You can become so caught up in those details that you feel you do not have time to think, much less think about something as monumental as changing your life. It seems so much easier to give in. "What else can you do?" others say. "That's just the way life is."

I do want to point out, friends, that time is of the essence. There is no time to waste, so don't complicate your lives unnecessarily. Keep it simple—in marriage, grief, joy, whatever. Even in ordinary things—your daily routines of shopping, and so on.

1 Corinthians 7:29–30 MSG

Never again will I make the simple into the complex. Something of true value does not become more valuable because it becomes complicated. Experience and conditions come and go; complications arise and fall away, but the simple action of God is eternal in the universe.

Donald Curtis

Hold it. God promised to give you an abundant life—a life full of richness and meaning and purpose. Instead, you are living a life of overabundance—too much of the things that do not count and too many hours attending to them.

Listen to what God is saying to you. Maybe, just maybe, he is trying to get you to hear these words in a whole different context: *It doesn't have to be this way.* You do not have to live your life according to artificial dictates imposed on you by the lifestyles of other people. Consider these options:

- Stores stay open twenty-four/seven to accommodate consumers, but you do not have to think of yourself in consumerist terms.

 Our life is frittered away by detail. Simplicity, simplicity, simplicity!
—Henry David Thoreau

- Instead of buying something that you like but do not need, you figure you can just go back to the store to visit it—but you probably will not, since you know it is not that important.

- Your salary enables you to live in an exclusive gated community and drive a luxury car, but you choose to live more simply so you can give more generously. You, not your six-figure salary, will determine where and how you live.

- Everyone you know is running their children ragged, convinced that if they do not participate in several sports and a half-dozen other activities, they will never succeed. Maybe they are right, but you are not so sure that all that running around is what God had in mind when he gave humans a childhood.

Too many people think in "either/or" terms. Either you live the typical lifestyle of a harried, rushed, stressed-out American, or you go back to nature and live in an unheated cabin with no plumbing, growing your own food, raising sheep for their wool, and making your own candles so you will have light. That is not simplicity; that is asceticism.

Simplifying your lifestyle can be accomplished to varying degrees and in incremental steps. The important thing to keep in mind is that the purpose of simplicity is to get rid of anything that stands in the way of serving God and other people. That can mean material things—often useless—that take time and money to maintain. It can mean a full schedule of activities that leave you little time to relax and recharge so you are prepared for the next thing God wants you to do. Or it can mean excessive debt that keeps you chained to a job that prevents you from following your heart on short-term mission trips.

Jesus modeled simplicity for his disciples and instructed them to follow his lead: "He commanded them to take nothing for the journey

interesting to note

Several years ago, a magazine devoted to a simpler lifestyle appeared on newsstands. Along with the requisite articles on decluttering the house and making meals in minutes were advertisements for trendy organizational products and must-have kitchen appliances. Keeping it simple had been redefined to include buying more stuff, at least in the pages of one magazine.

Don't think you need a lot of extra equipment for this. You are the equipment. No special appeals for funds. Keep it simple.

Mark 6:8 MSG

except a staff—no bag, no bread, no copper in their money belts—but to wear sandals, and not to put on two tunics" (Mark 6:8–9 NKJV). Simplicity was the order of the day.

what's essential

By doing something as simple as spending a few minutes each day in silence, in the presence of God, you can acquire a fresh perspective on your entire day. As your thoughts return to those moments of peace, you will begin to yearn for more. That may be just what you need to begin your journey toward simpler living.

DO take stock of the things that prevent you from living the life you want to live and begin eliminating them from your life.

DO start to take steps toward a simpler life now and work your way toward the bigger steps you are likely to want to take.

DON'T think of yourself as a consumer, no matter how any times you hear the media refer to people using that term.

DON'T feel as if your life will never change, that you are resigned to the rush-rush life of so many other people.

Honor Your Family

In public discussions about the family today, the hot topics tend to be family values, same-sex marriage, the high divorce rate, and to a lesser extent, cohabitation. But a more basic biblical concept gets much less ink, airtime, and bandwidth—that of honoring the individual members of your own family.

Honor your father and your mother as the LORD your God has commanded you. Then you will live a long time, and things will go well for you in the land that the LORD your God is going to give you.

Deuteronomy 5:16 NCV

English teachers everywhere know that there are two kinds of nouns, the abstract and the concrete. Simply put, you cannot detect anything represented by an abstract noun with your five senses; you cannot see, smell, hear, touch, or taste honesty, for example. But you can detect those things represented by concrete nouns; you can see, smell, hear, touch, or taste a juicy burger that has been roasting on an open barbecue grill. Not all concrete nouns, of course, can be perceived by all five senses; you cannot hear a table, and not many people would be inclined to taste one.

Seated around that table, waiting for those juicy burgers, are the individual members of a concrete group—your family. While politicians and religious leaders debate the future of the abstract

Family life is too intimate to be preserved by the spirit of justice. It can be sustained by a spirit of love which goes beyond justice.

Reinhold Niebuhr

institution known as the family, your concern is for the very real people who populate your home and your life, people with concrete physical needs like food, clothing, and shelter and abstract emotional needs for things like love, respect, and courtesy.

It is one thing to honor an abstract concept; of course you have high regard for the idea, and perhaps the ideal, of the family. But it is a whole different thing when you are expected to honor the concrete version—the pierced, tattooed daughter with a look of defiance on her face; the spouse whose voice is starting to grate on you after so many years of marriage; your own father, now elderly and talking nonstop about trivial, nonsensical things; the uncontrollable grandchild who cannot sit still for a minute and breaks everything he can get his hands on.

Call it a clan, call it a network, call it a tribe, call it a family: Whatever you call it, whoever you are, you need one.
—Jane Howard

That's an exaggerated version of a family, of course. Let's face it: it is not very hard to respect people who are courteous, clean-cut, quiet, and domesticated. But no family can boast of having members who consistently conduct themselves in that way, and that family's life would be pretty boring even if they could. The concrete family must navigate a messy, complex, dynamic, and sometimes rough-and-tumble existence together.

Meanwhile, you know your Bible well enough to know that you are supposed to honor your mother and father

(Deuteronomy 5:16 and elsewhere), respect and love your spouse (Ephesians 5), and love your children (Titus 2:4; Psalm 103:13). In addition, numerous verses refer to showing love and honor to everyone—and that includes your family.

So just how do you honor the individuals in this motley assemblage of distinct personalities? Ironically, in at least one place, the Bible assumes you are already doing this: "Do not speak angrily to an older man, but plead with him as if he were your father. Treat younger men like brothers, older women like mothers, and younger women like sisters. Always treat them in a pure way" (1 Timothy 5:1–3 NCV). Instead of having to tell Christians to treat family members with the kind of respect they show to other people, Paul feels the need to tell them to treat other people with the same respect they show to family members.

Honoring your family is actually much simpler than it sounds. Treat the members of your family the way you want to be treated—and in some respects, the way you treat a guest in your home. Obviously, family relationships are much more intimate than that of host and guest, but some of the same rules do apply. Listen to what they say. Say please and thank you. Do not

interesting to note

The entire Bible says a great deal about the physical family, but the New Testament extends the conversation to the spiritual family that is the church. God considers the spiritual family so important that he expects Christians to honor one another to the same extent that they honor their physical families.

We know what real love is because Jesus gave up his life for us. So we also ought to give up our lives for our brothers and sisters. If someone has enough money to live well and sees a brother or sister in need but shows no compassion— how can God's love be in that person?
1 John 3:16–17 NLT

belittle or demean. Make every effort to be accepting, patient, and kind.

Will you fail at times? Of course you will. Will you fail most of the time? Hopefully not. Courtesy is an acquired habit, and with practice, your success rate should far exceed your failure rate.

what's essential

As important as the abstract institution of the family is, it can only be as strong as the concrete individuals it is composed of. When you honor each member of your family in obedience to God, you are also contributing to the strength and success of the institution.

DO treat every member of your family with the kind of respect and courtesy you extend to people you'd like to impress—only do so with authenticity.

DO learn what the Bible says about how you should treat the individual members of your family.

DON'T expect members of your family to honor and respect you if you show little regard for honoring and respecting them.

DON'T treat your family well only when you are in public; your treatment of them in private is an even greater indication of how much respect you have for them.

Use Your Gifts and Talents

There's no question that God wants you to use the gifts and talents he has given you in ways that benefit other people and the entire church community. That is the easy part. But sometimes it is not that easy to determine just what your gifts and talents are, especially when you are new to a life of faith.

It is the one and only Spirit who distributes all these gifts. He alone decides which gift each person should have.

1 Corinthians 12:11 NLT

Newcomers to certain segments of the church are often baffled when they hear other Christians talk about using their gifts and talents. The uninitiated assume at first that what is being referred to is being gifted with a beautiful voice or having a special musical talent, in which case using those gifts and talents is a no-brainer; you join the musical team as a singer or an accompanist, and that is that.

But eventually, you figure out that they are talking about something called "spiritual gifts," and now you are confused. Apparently you have a gift but do not know it. Plus, you are being told it is time to find out what it is. You do not have a clue how to do that, even after looking over a list of spiritual gifts taken from the Bible.

To paraphrase Augustine, if you want to know your God-given gifts, first know that the purpose of spiritual gifts is to bring unity to the church.

Edward T. Welch

Maybe you've never heard of these gifts before, and you are feeling pressured to decide which gift you have before you understand exactly what each one is, like ordering a meal off a French-language menu when you do not understand a word of French. Or maybe you've read about spiritual gifts in the Bible or heard about them in a church you previously attended, but they weren't emphasized. Now, they seem to be incredibly important.

 The best way to discover and confirm which spiritual gift is yours is through serving.
—Donald Whitney

Yes, they are important. But you need to relax and understand that determining your spiritual gift often comes with time. Finding your gift is neither a treasure hunt nor a timed exam. God did not hide your gift in some dark and unexplored cave accessed only by an unlit path full of twists and turns and potential danger. Nor did he hand you a complicated multiple-choice exam and start his stopwatch. What he did was give you a desire to serve him, a passion for a particular area of service, and a knack for accomplishing the work that particular area of service requires.

Following is a list of a few gifts and their descriptions (in English!); see if any resonate with you.

- *Wisdom*—determining what God wants to say to the church as a whole or to individual members.

- *Faith*—having an extraordinary measure of trust in God, especially in situations where others have lost faith.

- *Healing*—restoring a sick or injured person to health and wholeness by drawing on God's power to heal.

- *Miracles*—performing what are known as "signs and wonders"—acts that could not be possible without God's supernatural power.

- *Tongues*—speaking in a language you do not know.

- *Administration*—keeping everything running smoothly in a church or other religious organization.

- *Helping*—serving others in practical ways.

The rest of this list is found in 1 Corinthians 12, and other gifts are mentioned elsewhere in the New Testament. Depending on the Bible translation you use, you may find that different words are used for some of the gifts, and the church you attend may define the terms in different and more detailed ways.

While it is important to become familiar with the gifts and understand what they are, racking your brain is the least effective way to determine what your specific gifts are. The most effective and productive way, and the way most useful to the church, is to start serving God as he leads and to the best of your ability. Your gift will emerge.

We all have different gifts, each of which came because of the grace God gave us. The person who has the gift of prophecy should use that gift in agreement with the faith.

Romans 12:6 NCV

One word of caution: do not desire a specific gift. If you have the gift of administration but you want the gift of healing, stick with administration. You are great at organizing things, right? That is the gift the Holy Spirit has given you—and you will be miserable when you fail at attempting those he hasn't given you.

what's essential

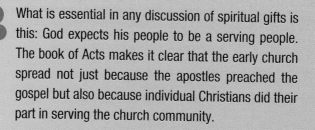

What is essential in any discussion of spiritual gifts is this: God expects his people to be a serving people. The book of Acts makes it clear that the early church spread not just because the apostles preached the gospel but also because individual Christians did their part in serving the church community.

DO learn all you can about the spiritual gifts mentioned throughout the New Testament.

DO ask God to help you discern what your gifts are and how they can best be used to serve the church community.

DON'T agonize over what your gift is or your gifts are; trust God to lead you into an area of service that is compatible with your gift.

DON'T desire a gift you do not have; you may fail at it, make yourself miserable, and possibly hurt others in the process.

Overcome the Fear of Failure

Lots of books, Web sites, newspaper columns, radio segments, television shows, advertisements, and commercials promise to deliver what so many people want—the secret to success. But as many a successful person has learned, one of the most important keys to success is no secret at all: never fear failure.

History books are filled with stories of people who failed—but not just the famous failures like Thomas Dewey, who lost the 1948 presidential election to Harry Truman despite a banner headline proclaiming otherwise. Actually, some of the historical figures who failed repeatedly include Abraham Lincoln, Thomas Edison, Isaac Newton, and Winston Churchill. But wait! These men were all successes, not failures, right? Yes and no. Yes, they were successes, but no, not always. Each one suffered numerous failures first. But each one refused to give in to failure, and each one ended up a success.

It turns out that failure is a great teacher. It teaches you what doesn't work. It teaches you

> Don't pick on people, jump on their failures, criticize their faults—unless, of course, you want the same treatment. Don't condemn those who are down; that hardness can boomerang. Be easy on people; you'll find life a lot easier.
>
> Luke 6:37 MSG

> Those who have failed miserably are often the first to see God's formula for success.
>
> Erwin W. Lutzer

tenacity and resilience and determination. If you are smart, it teaches you to keep trying until you get it right.

And if you are wise, it teaches you to continue trusting God despite your failures.

By that definition, David was a very wise man. As king, he should have been with his men on the battlefield. Instead, he was safe in his palace, or so it seemed. But danger lurked nearby in the form of lust. David lusted after Bathsheba, slept with her and got her pregnant, and then killed her husband to cover his tracks. And this was someone the Bible described as a man after God's own heart! But God let David know in no uncertain terms that he knew what David had done.

 We pay a heavy price for our fear of failure. It is a powerful obstacle to growth . . . There is no learning without some difficulty and fumbling. If you want to keep on learning, you must keep on risking failure all your life.
—John W. Gardner

Can you imagine how David must have felt when his sin was exposed? He had trusted God and tried to do right throughout his life, and there he was, caught in a web of deception and a killing, no less. He was by all accounts a moral failure. But David owned up to his failure, confessing his sin, accepting God's forgiveness, and doing right by Bathsheba. Throughout the rest of his life and his reign as king, he continued to trust God and succeeded in keeping the kingdom of Israel intact, despite numerous threats to its existence.

The stories of David and other biblical "failures"—Abraham, Moses, and Peter, to name a few—underscore the fact that failure is not final. Failure can turn out to be a mere bump in the road, but it can also be a springboard to much greater things, as it was in the case of Peter. Instead of defeating him, Peter's shame over his denial of Jesus seemed to be the final straw in his sometimes foolish life. Peter began to get his act together, and he went on to become one of the most prominent leaders in the early church.

It wasn't just Peter's shame that propelled him to leadership; it was God's love, grace, and forgiveness that gave Peter the strength he needed to keep going. Without that, Peter very well could have allowed his failure to make him fearful of ever taking another risk. Following Jesus had proven to be a risky venture. Given the Pharisees' opposition to Jesus and his followers prior to the resurrection, Peter must have realized the danger he would face if he continued to tell others about Jesus. But something had changed in him, and his single-minded mission—spreading the news that Jesus had risen from the dead—caused his fear of danger, and yet another failure, to evaporate.

interesting to note

Thomas Edison, who in 1879 developed a means of generating and distributing electric power worldwide, experienced more failures with his inventions than most scientists even attempt. "I have not failed," he maintained. "I've just found ten thousand ways that won't work." One biographer called him "the most influential figure of the millennium."

God did not give us a spirit that makes us afraid but a spirit of power and love and self-control.

2 Timothy 1:7 NCV

That single-minded focus has enabled many successful people to overcome their failures as well as their fear of failure. Failure means you've attempted something; fear of failure keeps you paralyzed. Once you give that fear to God, you can start moving forward again, taking risks, and maybe even drawing closer to success.

what's essential

Failure is not so much the opposite of success as it is an important component of it. Soichiro Honda, founder of Honda Motor Company, goes so far as to say that failure makes up 99 percent of any successful venture. Seen that way, failure can be a positive stepping-stone to success.

DO ask God to help you overcome your fear of failure.

DO get back up after every failure and keep attempting whatever it is you are trying to succeed at doing.

DON'T allow the fear of failure to paralyze you and prevent you from taking risks and moving closer to success.

DON'T forget what so many successful people have learned—that one of the keys to success is resisting the fear of failure.

How Do I Live My Life Every Day?

WONDER

You quieted the raging oceans with their pounding waves and silenced the shouting of the nations. Those who live at the ends of the earth stand in awe of your wonders. From where the sun rises to where it sets, you inspire shouts of joy.

Psalm 65:7–8 NLT

Every object in nature is impressed with God's footsteps, and every day repeats the wonders of creation.

Thomas Guthrie

Two things fill me with constantly increasing admiration and awe, the longer and more earnestly I reflect on them: the starry heavens without and the moral law within.

Immanuel Kant

Nurture the Faith of Others

When you look back on your life with God, do you see the faces of people who helped you along the way? It is likely you do. Most people develop a strong relationship with God because someone has nurtured their faith. Who is looking to you to be shown how to have a faith-filled relationship with God?

You may not know the answer to that question right now, because it never occurred to you to ask it. But if someone is hoping you will help nurture their faith, how would you go about it? This is a crucial question to ask. Throughout the New Testament, church leaders emphasized how important it was for more mature Christians to teach and train those who were new to the faith. Paul specifically told Timothy to "be ready at all times, and tell people what they need to do" (2 Timothy 4:2 NCV).

If that seems intimidating, it needn't be. Nurturing the faith of others doesn't require a theological education—no one in the early church had one either. Two things it does require, however, are your own unflinching faith in God and a genuine willingness to encourage others in their own faith. As Irish pastor Derick Bingham put it, "The encourager, no matter how dark the day, always brings a message of hope. Those who encourage . . . are in effect only beggars telling other beggars where to find help." When you think of yourself as a beggar bringing hope and pointing the way, it is hard to feel intimidated by the task before you.

And the task requires commitment. Helping others grow in faith takes time and energy; you are part mentor, part teacher, part friend, and all those parts add up to make you a spiritual role model. As such, it is your responsibility to set an example. That shouldn't intimidate you either, because if you are already living an authentic life before God, you do not need to change a thing.

We never grow too old to be mentored or to be a mentor . . . The torch must be passed continuously from one generation to the next.
—Curtis C. Thomas

But where do you start? There is so much involved in a life of faith that the thought of conveying that to another person can be overwhelming. But remember—this isn't a lecture or a Bible study. This is a relationship, and you start by getting to know each other better and building trust in the process. As you do, you will get a better handle on what your friend expects from you—and he or she will get a better handle on whether that expectation is realistic.

Some things to keep in mind:

- *Pray—and keep on praying.* Any close relationship can be challenging. This one requires special care and handling. Ask God to keep your motives pure and your heart turned toward him.

- *Your purpose is to help strengthen his or her relationship with God.* Remember, you are supposed to point the way, not get in the way. You say something brilliant, but instead of silently thanking God for the insight you just shared and leaving it at that, you give in to the temptation to build on that brilliance. Now you are operating in your own strength rather than God's, and you are interfering with God's interaction with your friend.

- *You are not expected to know everything, not that you ever could.* If you do not know the answer to your friend's question, admit it, no matter how basic the question is. Consider the situation an opportunity for the two of you to open your Bibles and try to find the answer together. If you cannot, assure your friend that you will get back to her with the answer.

- *Offer hope and encouragement.* Newcomers to a life of faith sometimes experience disappointment with themselves and other Christians, and setbacks in their efforts to please God. Encourage your friend to keep her focus on God and remind her that God loves her no matter what.

• *Relax.* Yes, this is a big responsibility. Just remember to keep your focus on God, and remind yourself that God loves *you* no matter what.

what's essential

Be careful not to take on the role of a counselor unless you are trained to do so. If you sense that a person needs professional help, refer him to a trained counselor. Be careful also to offer advice only about how to grow in the faith. Decline to offer an opinion on family problems, for example.

DO prepare yourself now to help someone else along in their relationship with God—because that is what he expects his followers to do.

DO be a full-time encourager to others, pointing the way to God and offering hope that their faith will grow.

DON'T interfere with your friend's relationship with God; you are there to help it along while also staying out of the way.

DON'T attempt to solve your friend's problems; do not offer advice on any matter apart from those related to her faith in God.

Enlarge Your Sphere of Influence

For many Christians, their church is also the center of their social life—not necessarily the building but the people who attend. That is only natural; you have a great deal in common with your friends at church. But if you want to have an impact on your community, you will have to widen your area of influence.

Do you realize that you are a person of influence? Maybe you hear that description and think it applies only to the rich and famous and powerful, but that is not true. Unless you are a hermit, you influence others as you go about your daily life. The question is, what kind of influence are you having on those around you—especially those outside your faith community?

Some Christians are hesitant to step outside their circle of friends from church. They may have good reasons for the way they feel—they may be concerned, for example, about falling back into an unhealthy lifestyle they left behind years before. But people are watching, and they see that those Christians are isolating themselves from the

There is no power on earth that can neutralize the influence of a high, simple and useful life.

Booker T. Washington

rest of the community. Whether they are right or not, what they see is people who seem to be afraid to mingle with the rest of society or who feel superior to those outside their clique. It doesn't matter whether that is a valid observation; their perception is their reality, and what they perceive is not exactly a reflection of God's love for them.

Those who love God are called to bring light to those who live in spiritual darkness. You cannot do that if you remain in the shadows, never letting the light of God shine through you to those who desperately need it. Your church friends may represent your comfort zone, but God did not call you to be comfortable; he called you to be obedient. And that means taking his love to those in your sphere of influence.

 Blessed is the influence of one true, loving human soul on another.
—George Eliot

If that sphere needs to be enlarged, here are some suggestions that might make that expansion a bit easier:

- Do not be afraid that your new acquaintances will have a negative influence on you; be confident that you will have a positive influence on them. Fear should never control your life. God should.

- Pay more attention than usual to people you've had only casual interaction with up to now—cashiers, receptionists, and so forth. Make eye contact. Engage them in a brief conversation when it is appropriate. You may be amazed at their reaction; they may be accustomed to being treated as if they are invisible, and you've just shaken things up. You have no idea the difference you could make in their day.

- Get out into your community—and not just by getting involved in activities that feel safe to you. Your fellow golfers certainly need your influence, but it wouldn't hurt to spread some of that influence while you are shooting pool at the local sports bar either.

- Listen, listen, and listen some more. You are building relationships. This is no time to preach, judge, correct, argue, or teach. The more closely you listen, the more readily you can determine what another person's spiritual needs are, and the more apt you are to remember details that you can ask about the next time you get together, conveying respect and a genuine interest in the person's life.

- Be friendly. Be helpful. Do not look at people as "prospects"—potential converts. Look at them as potential friends to whom you can show genuine concern, compassion, and the love of God.

Jesus told his followers, "You should be a light for other people. Live so that they will see the good things you do and will praise your Father in heaven" (Matthew 5:16 NCV). You can have a profound effect on other people by being an example of the love of God on earth—but they need to see your example and sense God's love emanating from you.

what's essential

 God reveals himself to people in any number of ways. One of the primary ways, though, is through his people, spreading his love to those who have no idea how to find it otherwise. Every time you interact with people who do not know God, you are a part of God's purpose for his people.

DO step outside your comfort zone and begin to interact with people with whom you seem to have little in common.

DO see yourself as a person of influence—and make sure that influence serves to show people the love of God.

DON'T treat people as if they are invisible by failing to make eye contact or failing to pay close attention to them.

DON'T forget that people are watching you and—whether it is fair or not—judging the extent of God's love by the love his followers show to others.

Listen to Words of Wisdom

One thing that seems to be in short supply worldwide is wisdom. But there is no need for that. From the very beginning, God imparted his wisdom to his people so they would know the right way to live and be able to teach others to do the same. His wisdom is every bit as valid for today's world as it was in the beginning.

Wisdom is the most important thing; so get wisdom. If it costs everything you have, get understanding.

Proverbs 4:7 NCV

Having wisdom does not mean that you understand all of God's ways; it means that you respond to life God's way. The better you know the Bible, the wiser you will become.

Ken Sande

Many Christians wonder why people are so blind to what they believe is the ultimate truth about life and how to live it. They've been reading their Bibles for so long that looking at the world from God's perspective has become second nature to them. Why, they ask, can't everyone understand the very basics of who God is and how he wants people to live and why they are here in the first place?

The short answer is that not everyone has been reading the Bible or believing that its content is relevant to today's world. The long answer is much too long to include here; suffice it to say that it has to do with science and technology and medical marvels that understandably cause skeptics of religion to place their faith in the wisdom of humanity.

This comes as no surprise to God. He has been dealing with skeptics since the dawn of time. And he has been counting on his people to counter the wisdom of humanity with his wisdom. He knows that some people will always try to set themselves far above him, believing that thousands of years of civilization have made them much smarter than God.

Authentic wisdom begins when we understand that God is to be the object of our devotion, our adoration, and our reverence.
—R. C. Sproul

Here's what God had to say about that: "My thoughts are not like your thoughts. Your ways are not like my ways. Just as the heavens are higher than the earth, so are my ways higher than your ways and my thoughts higher than your thoughts" (Isaiah 55:8–9 NCV). That is what sets God's wisdom apart from humanity's; God's ways of thinking and doing are far superior to those of people. Believing differently—applying to God distinctly human ways of thinking and behaving—is an error people have been making for millennia. God will have none of that, as he once told those who had forgotten him: "These things you have done and I kept silence; you thought that I was just like you; I will reprove you and state the case in order before your eyes" (Psalm 50:21 NASB).

So here's one item in the case that God was making. Human wisdom seems to make sense to people, so they choose that over God's wisdom—but it ends in death (Proverbs 14:12). Furthermore, wisdom begins with respect for God (Psalm 111:9–10), so those who have no respect for him adhere to a false understanding of wisdom from the outset. In Isaiah 29:14, God announces that the wisdom and intelligence of the wise and intelligent will pass away, which later prompted Paul to ask, "So where does this leave the philosophers, the scholars, and the world's brilliant debaters? God has made the wisdom of this world look foolish" (1 Corinthians 1:20 NLT).

Fortunately, God did not leave his people without a source of his wisdom. The Bible contains a wealth of wisdom, from Genesis straight through to Revelation. The problem is not that people are left to their own devices when it comes to making wise decisions, spending their money wisely, treating difficult situations with wisdom, and so forth; the problem is that people are looking for wisdom in all the wrong places. Either they've rejected the Bible as a source of wisdom, or they do not realize what a storehouse of wisdom it is.

As you read the Bible, pay particular attention to the underlying wisdom on each page and apply what you've read to your everyday life. Every time you make a move that reflects the wisdom of God, you are helping others see that God's wisdom works. Human wisdom cannot compete with the wisdom of God—neither will it last.

what's essential

God provided people with a treasury of wisdom. Mentally agreeing with his wisdom is a first step, but the critical subsequent steps involve learning from it and applying it to your life. Without that application, God's wisdom cannot help you avoid foolish mistakes as you navigate your way through life.

DO learn to recognize the distinction between God's wisdom and humanity's so you can immediately apply God's wisdom to any situation.

DO ask God for a deeper understanding of his wisdom.

DON'T expect people who have no knowledge of the Bible to think or act according to the wisdom found in it.

DON'T follow advice that seems to make sense without first determining whether it lines up with the wisdom God has given you.

Deal with Your Past

As a 1970s radio personality, Ruth Elizabeth Curtis was so wild off the air that a colleague—shock jock and extreme bad boy Howard Stern—told her to clean up her act. Ruth's lifestyle involved sex, drugs, and rock and roll to the max. Talk about a past! But how she turned out is just as shocking.

Ruth's present bears no resemblance to her past. Nearly thirty years ago, she traded cocaine and one-night stands for an offer she couldn't refuse: God's complete, unconditional, inexplicable, life-changing forgiveness. Today, she ministers to women worldwide, including many of her fellow FBGs—Former Bad Girls. Actually, you may already be familiar with Ruth Curtis and her ministry. She's novelist Liz Curtis Higgs, with more than three million Christian books in print and a speaking ministry that spans the globe.

Like Ruth—or Liz—many Christians have a sordid past of their own making. Others feel unwarranted shame over terrible abuse that was inflicted on them. Some cringe over the unethical, unwise, and unkind acts that litter their past. But

Brethren, I do not count myself to have apprehended; but one thing I do, forgetting those things which are behind and reaching forward to those things which are ahead, I press toward the goal for the prize of the upward call of God in Christ Jesus.

Philippians 3:13–14 NKJV

God does not want to remove your memories; he wants to redeem them. He wants to transform them into something good, something that will make you more like Jesus.

Robert D. Jones

many, if not most, of those Christians turned to God precisely because of their troubled histories. In him, they found forgiveness and healing.

For some people, though, the memories return—or they never leave. Maybe you are among those haunted by memories of a past that God forgave but you never forgot. Trying to forget the past is a pointless endeavor.

But there is a way to confront your past, learn from it, and move on: by asking God to redeem it. Stop trying to forget it; stop trying to live your life as if it never happened. Instead, pick your past up again and hand it over to God. Let his hands transform your past into something useful, such as a ministry to others whose difficult experiences mirror yours.

We have to learn to commit not only the future but also the past to the Lord.
—Daniel Fuller

That's what God did for Liz Curtis Higgs. After turning her life over to God in 1982, Liz left her past in God's hands, went on with her new life, and eventually started to speak publicly and write Christian books. Her past found its way into both areas of ministry. Women she calls "Former Bad Girls" were drawn by her transparency, and her life inspired them to also turn to God for forgiveness and healing. Her novels found a huge following, but so did three of her best-known nonfiction titles: *Bad Girls of the Bible, Slightly Bad Girls of the Bible,* and of course, *Really Bad Girls of the Bible.* There is no question that God has redeemed Liz's past.

You do not have to become a best-selling author to have your past redeemed. You do not even have to have a particularly sordid past. Memories that pale in comparison to Liz's can nevertheless be painful and even traumatic to the person who harbors them.

Not surprisingly, dealing with your past starts with prayer. If you leave God out of the process, you open yourself up to a host of negative and potentially harmful emotions. Here's one path that process could follow:

- Admit to your past. Denial is never healthy.

- Ask God to begin healing you as you confront your past.

- Ask God to forgive you of your wrongdoing or for the strength to forgive someone who abused you (if the abuse was recent, trust God to enable you to forgive when you are ready).

- Ask God to redeem your past and use it in a way that will draw people to him.

- Finally, forget it—do not dwell on it—and move on. It is in God's hands now. When the time is right, he'll show you how to use your past in its redeemed form to minister to others.

If the wounds and the memories are still fresh, healing may seem impossible. It isn't. How can you be sure? Because Jesus said this about the seemingly impossible: "For people this is impossible, but for God all things are possible" (Matthew 19:26 NCV).

what's essential

Regret has a significant bearing on your present and your future. It can be a powerful reminder of things to avoid, but it can also keep you from enjoying the present. Getting rid of anything, such as regret, that weighs you down is essential if you want to serve God to the fullest.

DO give your past to God, entrust him with it, and go on with your life until he brings it up again.

DO believe that with God, all things are possible—including the transformation of your past experiences into a means of drawing people into a relationship with him.

DON'T deny the wrong you've done or the wrong done to you; denial is a barrier to the healing you need to experience.

DON'T consider anything you've done to be immune to God's forgiveness. Likewise, do not consider anything too trivial to take to God; if it bothers you, it is important to him.

Create a Life of Balance

If you were to make a list of every area of life that requires your attention, you'd likely be writing for a very long time. Balancing work, spouse, children, church, extended family, rest, exercise, health, friends, neighbors, pets, hobbies—it's all too much to even think about. How can you balance all that?

Trying to balance their lives—actually, just thinking about it—is enough to make grown-ups cry. Life coaches, pop psychologists, and Christian leaders urge people to keep everything in their lives running smoothly simply by figuring out how to give just the right amount of time and attention to all the items on that imaginary list above. Most often, this takes the form of a pie chart, with each slice representing one of those items and the presenter breaking everything down into a fine-tuned plan for organizing your life.

There's more than one problem with that. No one's life can be that uniformly segmented. The labels on the slices may bear no resemblance to the way you think about your life. Plus, someone left off all the toppings! A single slice of your pie may be piled high with toppings and have oily cheese sliding over onto slices where it doesn't belong. Isn't there a better way to look at this?

There is. See if this works for you. Instead of compartmentalizing your life in a way that feels artificial to you, approach the image of a balanced life with broader strokes, trusting God to work out the details that will move you toward greater balance. Your life may be much too fluid to think of it in segments. If God is in control of all your life, then trying to micromanage individual segments is pointless. If you instead apply God's principles for sound living to your entire life, then your life cannot help but fall into just the right balance at the right time.

 Balance, peace, and joy are the fruit of a successful life. It starts with recognizing your talents and finding ways to serve others by using them.
—Thomas Kinkade

You are already familiar with the concept that will make this "broad strokes" approach work: it is your conscience. Do you really need a written plan to let you know when you are working too much? Probably not. What you have is a moral compass inside you that helps you interpret and apply God's principles to every situation. That compass lets you know, without a doubt, that it is time to lay your work aside and do something that will balance out your workday: play with your kids if you are

interesting to note

Ecclesiastes 7:15–22 catalogs the pitfalls of an unbalanced life. In the NIV, readers are even warned not to be too righteous or too wise. "The man who fears God will avoid all extremes," according to verse 18. Finally, there is this advice in verses 21–22: "Do not pay attention to every word people say, or you may hear your servant cursing you—for you know in your heart that many times you yourself have cursed others."

The Kingdom of God is not a matter of what we eat or drink, but of living a life of goodness and peace and joy in the Holy Spirit.

Romans 14:17 NLT

a parent, have some fun with your friends if you are not, go home and read, visit someone you have not seen in a while. Your compass also alerts you that it is time to stop playing and get back to work, or that it is time to do a different kind of work—giving some serious attention to your spiritual life, perhaps.

But if your conscience is such a great guide, why does your life seem so out of whack? Well, your conscience can only tell you what to do; it cannot make you do it. Catch your thoughts the next time you feel a nudge to change direction—to go home, say, instead of staying at work "just one more hour." If you get up and go, your response to the compass is in fine working order. But if you start justifying your need to stay—"Joe needs this report first thing in the morning!"—then it is time to start paying closer attention to your conscience.

If none of this resonates with you—if you are the type who thrives on organizational methods and succeeds at using them—you will have no lack of books and online resources to help you balance out all those slices of your personal pie chart. The rest of you can be confident that God will intervene when your life veers toward imbalance: "Your ears will hear a word behind you, 'This is the way, walk in it,' whenever you turn to the right or to the left" (Isaiah 30:21 NASB.)

what's essential

Consider using Micah 6:8 as your guiding principle for a balanced life: "He has told you, O man, what is good; and what does the LORD require of you but to do justice, to love kindness, and to walk humbly with your God?" (NASB). By serving as a reminder of what is essential in God's sight, that verse has helped many people restore balance to their lives.

DO remember that no one ever "arrives" at a permanently balanced life; it is enough that you are moving toward it.

DO trust God to let you know when your life is approaching imbalance and guide you in the new direction you should take.

DON'T let your mind do battle with your conscience when it is clear to you that your conscience is trying to get you to do the right thing.

DON'T become discouraged when your life seems out of whack; use that awareness to take steps toward achieving balance.

How Do I Live My Life Every Day?

HOPE

Our soul waits for the LORD; He is our help and our shield. For our heart shall rejoice in Him, because we have trusted in His holy name. Let Your mercy, O LORD, be upon us, just as we hope in You.

Psalm 33:20–22 NKJV

There are no hopeless situations; there are only people who have grown hopeless about them.

Clare Boothe Luce

When you say a situation or person is hopeless, you are slamming the door in the face of God.

Charles E. Allen

Cultivate Healthy Friendships

Friend is a word used loosely these days. Some people have hundreds—or even thousands—of "friends" on MySpace, Facebook, and similar sites, friends they've never met. But the relationships they've established with their on-line friends fall short of the real thing. Their interaction is networking—not friendship.

The term "online friends" may prove to be the ultimate oxymoron. They may be online, but they are not friends. True friendships require a host of qualities in each other that simply cannot be confirmed in cyberspace, like trustworthiness and authenticity. Granted, the term is largely used as shorthand, an easy way to describe your interaction. Just do not make the mistake of thinking your social networking buddies are actually friends.

Friends are real live flesh-and-blood people whom you can trust and be your real live flesh-and-blood self with. Friendships are deep commitments with those people. Friendships take time and energy to develop and time and energy to maintain. They cannot be taken lightly if you want them to last.

No longer do I call you servants, for a servant does not know what his master is doing; but I have called you friends, for all things that I heard from My Father I have made known to you.

John 15:15 NKJV

The glory of friendship is not the outstretched hand, not the kindly smile, not the joy of companionship; it is the spiritual inspiration that comes to one when he discovers that someone believes in him and is willing to trust him with his friendship.

Ralph Waldo Emerson

Genuine friends have these traits in common:

- *They listen.* "This you know, my beloved brethren. But everyone must be quick to hear, slow to speak and slow to anger" (James 1:19 NASB).

- *They comfort.* "A friend loves you all the time, and a brother helps in time of trouble" (Proverbs 17:17 NCV).

- *They counsel.* "So how should I prepare to come to you? As a severe disciplinarian who makes you toe the mark? Or as a good friend and counselor who wants to share heart-to-heart with you? You decide" (1 Corinthians 4:21 MSG).

 Friendship is born at that moment when one person says to another: "What! You, too? I thought I was the only one."
—C. S. Lewis

- *They do not complain.* "Friends, don't complain about each other. A far greater complaint could be lodged against you, you know. The Judge is standing just around the corner" (James 5:9 MSG).

- *They are committed.* "Now when he [David] had finished speaking to Saul, the soul of Jonathan was knit to the soul of David, and Jonathan loved him as his own soul" (1 Samuel 18:1 NKJV).

- *They are faithful and loyal.* "The man of many friends [a friend of all the world] will prove himself a bad friend, but there is a friend who sticks closer than a brother" (Proverbs 18:24 AMP).

- *They forgive.* "Be alert. If you see your friend going wrong, correct him. If he responds, forgive him. Even if it's personal against you and repeated seven times through the day, and seven times he says, 'I'm sorry, I won't do it again,' forgive him" (Luke 17:3–4 MSG).

- *They help.* "Two are better than one, because they have a good return for their work: If one falls down, his friend can help him up. But pity the man who falls and has no one to help him up!" (Ecclesiastes 4:9–10 NIV).

- *They make each other better.* "You use steel to sharpen steel, and one friend sharpens another" (Proverbs 27:17 MSG).

Friends are also available to each other. If you have a genuine need, call a friend for help, and your friend says she cannot help, that is understandable. But if she says she cannot help time after time, you need to reevaluate your relationship.

There's a flip side to friendship, of course. Friends let you down. They betray you. They abandon you. They disappoint you. They get busy. When good friends hurt you, it can be difficult to trust again. The temptation is strong to forget about friendship. You have enough acquaintances to spend time with; you do not need to make yourself vulnerable again.

Think carefully about that. Friendship creates an intimate bond and a safe place where you can

interesting to note

Proverbs also warns you how not to behave toward friends. It cautions you not to gossip (17:9); argue pointlessly (17:14); overstay your welcome (25:17); interfere inappropriately (26:17); tease (26:18–19); or abandon your friend (27:10).

Greater love has no one than this, than to lay down one's life for his friends. You are My friends if you do whatever I command you.
John 15:13–14 NKJV

be yourself without fear of judgment or ridicule. One person breaking that trust is not an accurate prediction of what will happen in your next friendship. Having someone in your life who knows you as you are and loves you anyway is a priceless gift—one that comes with both knowing God and having a real live flesh-and-blood friend.

what's essential

Do not be surprised when your friendships are tested. Misunderstandings, for example, can separate the best of friends. It is essential that you and your friend be transparent in the way you communicate with each other before problems arise. When they do, you will find it much easier to set things straight.

DO remember that friendship is a two-way street; you always need to try to be a better friend to others than they are to you.

DO take the biblical view of friendship into account as you begin to form a friendship with someone new.

DON'T let your disappointment with former friends keep you from developing close friendships now and in the future.

DON'T be deceived into thinking that your social networking friends are true friends. They may be completely trustworthy and honest—but you cannot know that for certain.

Give Generously

Americans are known for their generosity. In 2006, they gave a record $295 billion to charitable organizations. That may seem impressive, but it represents only an average of 2.6 percent of the income of each person. Is that generosity? Or is it simply giving?

Listen carefully to what I am saying—and be wary of the shrewd advice that tells you how to get ahead in the world on your own. Giving, not getting, is the way. Generosity begets generosity. Stinginess impoverishes.

Mark 4:24–25 MSG

In 1995, an eighty-seven-year-old woman in failing health was forced to retire from the work she had done for seventy-five years—taking in washing and ironing for other people in her hometown of Hattiesburg, Mississippi. It was time, she figured, to get her affairs in order. She did not have much in the way of material possessions, just a small bungalow her uncle had given her. She did not even own a car and made the two-mile round-trip to the grocery on foot, pushing a shopping cart.

Well, there was that money in the bank, the money she had saved over the years, a few dollars at a time. She wanted to give it away, but she did not quite understand how much she had. So a bank official spread ten dimes on his desk and asked her

Generosity is impossible apart from our love of God and of His people. But with such love, generosity not only is possible but inevitable.

John MacArthur

how she would divide them up among those she wanted to give her money to. She decided to give three dimes to her church, two to her family, and the remaining five to a school down the street.

That school was the University of Southern Mississippi (USM), and each dime represented $30,000 of Oseola McCarty's life savings. The check for $150,000 that she handed over to the university would go to a scholarship fund for underprivileged students. Her contribution made national headlines, and soon matching contributions started to pour into the school.

That's generosity, to be sure. In all, McCarty gave a whopping 80 percent of her life savings to charity. And her generosity inspired others to make additional contributions to the Oseola McCarty Scholarship Fund.

 When we come to the end of life, the question will be, "How much have you given?" not "How much have you gotten?"
—George Sweeting

But there is more to Oseola McCarty's story:

• McCarty, an African-American, was born sometime in 1908. She wanted to become a nurse, but the USM did not admit African-Americans when she was old enough to enroll.

• She quit school in the sixth grade to care for her ailing aunt. She continued to take in ironing, which she had been doing for several years.

• She lived so frugally that her Bible was held together with tape; one of Paul's letters to the Corinthians was particularly inclined to fall out.

- People who knew her personally—she died in 1999—universally described her as an uncomplaining, gentle, and welcoming person.

That's generosity of spirit. Oseola McCarty never returned to school because of the limited difference a high school diploma would have made to an African-American girl at the time. She wanted to become a nurse, but even if she'd had a diploma, USM would have refused to admit her because of the color of her skin. But she bore no grudge against USM, the school she chose to leave her money to.

What is more, she gave of herself by taking care of her aunt—an enormous responsibility for a thirteen-year-old girl. Again, no one ever knew her to complain. She had become a combination washerwoman and caregiver at a young age.

And she denied herself many household conveniences—not to mention a new Bible!—so others could benefit from her disciplined savings habit. In fact, it took several bankers to convince her to buy an air conditioner in hot and humid Mississippi—but not until three years before her death.

Keep Oseola McCarty's story in mind as you consider generosity as an essential component of everyday living. Generosity includes financial

interesting to note

A recent University of Michigan study reported a link between generosity of spirit and a long life, with elderly men who gave emotional or practical help to others proving to live longer than men who received emotional or practical help. Helping, it seems, reduces stress and strengthens the immune system.

Out of the most severe trial, their overflowing joy and their extreme poverty welled up in rich generosity.
2 Corinthians 8:2 NIV

giving, but that is not all it includes. When you give generously of your time and your energy—and give up your right to complain and feel resentful, as she did—you exemplify generosity of spirit, a quality so rare that it leads off newscasts, makes page-one headlines, and inspires others to give generously as well.

what's essential

Some people tithe—give 10 percent of their income to God—but give little thought to the remaining 90 percent. By asking God to bless all that you have, show you how to use it, and do what he says with it, you are likely to find yourself giving a much higher percentage, with plenty to spare.

DO give generously of your time, your money, your energy, and your other resources.

DO volunteer as much as you can, because the need is great and the number of people who are able to volunteer is shrinking.

DON'T confuse basic giving with generosity; generosity involves sacrificial giving, often of yourself.

DON'T give to get—though you may discover that the more you give, the more you do in fact get.

Get a Handle on Money

Ask any financial counselor how to gain control over your money, and she'll tell you this: set up a budget and stick to it. The first part makes sense, but the second part trips you up. Your personal history confirms that. So what do you do? Well, what if you scrapped the idea of a budget altogether?

In the financial world, the notion of failing to maintain a budget is akin to blasphemy in the religious world. One definition of *blasphemy*, according to the eleventh edition of *Merriam-Webster's Collegiate Dictionary*, is this: "irreverence toward something considered sacred or inviolable." Can you think of anything in the financial world that is considered more "sacred or inviolable" than a budget?

A budget is essential in the business world, but it doesn't have to be with regard to your personal finances. However, if you already have a workable personal or household budget and can stick to it, by all means continue what you are doing. It seldom makes sense to switch gears on a machine that is running smoothly.

Why do you spend money for what is not bread, and your wages for what does not satisfy? Listen carefully to Me, and eat what is good, and delight yourself in abundance.

Isaiah 55:2 NASB

The real measure of our wealth is how much we would be worth if we lost all our money.

J. H. Jowett

What's the alternative to a budget? Simply this: arranging your finances according to biblical principles. The Bible says a lot about money; there you have a wealth of financial wisdom at your fingertips.

God can have our money and not have our hearts, but He cannot have our hearts without having our money.
—Kent Hughes

Several portions of the Bible speak a great deal about finances in particular, such as the books of Proverbs and Ecclesiastes and several of Jesus' parables. As you read the book of Proverbs, for example, you will find these pithy sayings about specific issues concerning money:

- *Greed.* "Sinners will fall into their own traps; they will only catch themselves! All greedy people end up this way; greed kills selfish people" (1:18–19 NCV).

- *Laziness.* "He who has a slack hand becomes poor, but the hand of the diligent makes rich" (10:4 NKJV).

- *Giving.* "The one who blesses others is abundantly blessed; those who help others are helped" (11:25 MSG).

- *Trusting in wealth.* "Those who trust in riches will be ruined, but a good person will be healthy like a green leaf" (11:28 NCV).

- *Hoarding money.* "A thick bankroll is no help when life falls apart, but a principled life can stand up to the worst" (11:4 MSG).

- *Hard work.* "Those who work their land will have plenty of food, but the one who chases empty dreams is not wise" (12:11 NCV).

- *Easy money.* "Money that comes easily disappears quickly, but money that is gathered little by little will grow" (13:11 NCV).

- *Borrowing.* "The rich rules over the poor, and the borrower is servant to the lender" (22:7 NKJV).

Can you see how being guided by those principles would simplify your financial planning? And that is just a start. Combine the financial wisdom from Proverbs with that found in the rest of the Bible, and you have a winning formula for financial responsibility. One example is found in Isaiah 55:2, the verse at the beginning of this chapter. Spend your money on the essentials, like food, and not on things that do not bring satisfaction; find delight in God's abundance. Add that to the list above, keep adding similar verses as you find them in the Bible, and you have a storehouse of wisdom that cannot compare with a budget you will never follow.

It doesn't matter whether you are poor, wealthy, or somewhere in between; God's principles work for everyone. There is nothing wrong with wealth; there is everything wrong with making the accumulation of wealth the goal of your

interesting to note

Stewardship has become a distinctly Christian concept. It refers to the understanding that people actually own nothing for themselves. God gave people the earth and all it contains, and they are to be wise caretakers of it, just as a king's steward is responsible for taking care of the royal possessions.

Lust for money brings trouble and nothing but trouble. Going down that path, some lose their footing in the faith completely and live to regret it bitterly ever after.

1 Timothy 6:10 MSG

life. There is no shame in poverty; there is shame in refusing to work to provide for your family. And there is nothing wrong with the in-between; contentment is more easily attained when you are free from the despair that comes with surviving poverty and the headaches that come with managing wealth.

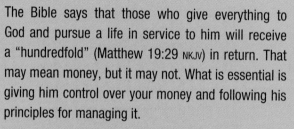

what's essential

 The Bible says that those who give everything to God and pursue a life in service to him will receive a "hundredfold" (Matthew 19:29 NKJV) in return. That may mean money, but it may not. What is essential is giving him control over your money and following his principles for managing it.

DO search the Bible for more financial principles and incorporate them into your life.

DO spend less than you earn, a principle gleaned from the complete teaching on finances in the Bible.

DON'T spend your money on things that do not satisfy, but rely on God and his abundance to satisfy you.

DON'T make the accumulation of wealth your life's goal, as so many have done.

Accept Who You Are

Imagine waking up, looking outside, and telling God, "I really think you did a lousy job with this world you created. I mean, look at it! It is a mess! It cannot even decide whether or not to rain!" Sound ridiculous? That may well be how you sound to God when you criticize one of his greatest creations—you.

You're blessed when you're content with just who you are— no more, no less. That's the moment you find yourselves proud owners of everything that can't be bought.
Matthew 5:5 MSG

If you have trouble accepting yourself on any level—the way you look, the mistakes you make, the sound of your voice, the family you came from—you are not alone. If you could read the thoughts of some of the most beautiful, handsome, talented, accomplished, successful people in the world, you might be astonished to discover that their problems with self-acceptance are not much different from yours.

How can that be? How can people who seem to have it all together be so self-critical, so unsure of themselves—so much like ordinary people? The answer to that one is easy. They've fallen into the trap of comparing themselves to others who they think are more beautiful, handsome, talented, accomplished, or successful. Think about it. If you

To despise yourself is really to despise God who made you the person you are. To accept yourself is to accept that he has done a good job on you.
David Matthew

do not like the shape of your nose, it is because you've seen a nose, or many noses, that you like better. Without that image of a better nose, it wouldn't occur to you that yours is unattractive.

The simple cure for your inability to accept your flawed self, then, would be to stop making comparisons—except for the fact that not doing so may sound simple but is exceedingly difficult as a first step. You will need a better plan than that.

 Once we come into peace with ourselves, we will begin to come into peace with others. If we learn to accept and like ourselves, we will accept and like others.
—Joyce Meyer

In fact, you will need the best plan of all—turning to God. If you believe that he made you to be who you are, with all your unique characteristics, including that nose you do not like, then he is the One you should be talking to. Tell him how you feel about yourself. Tell him about all your weaknesses, imperfections, embarrassing habits, anything and everything you do not like about yourself. It is okay to do this. He has heard it all before, but he will listen to you as if he is hearing it for the first time.

So what just happened? Do not be surprised if you experienced an overwhelming sense of God's love and acceptance. Were you expecting a rebuke? A taste of his anger? Here is the thing: God understands. He understands his people—their pain, their insecurities, their tendency to criticize and hate themselves. He wants to free them—to free you—from the prison of self-loathing.

Make no mistake about it—people who cannot accept themselves are in a kind of prison. They are trapped inside their own heads, unable to interact normally with the outside world. While others are talking, they are wondering if the last thing they said sounded stupid, if the clothes they are wearing are appropriate for the occasion, if they even belong with this group of people at all. If you have trouble accepting yourself, pay attention to your thoughts the next time you are in a group setting. It is highly likely that they will sound a lot like the ones you just read.

The freedom that comes with accepting yourself is immeasurable, because the results are so profound. Your relationship with God will improve dramatically when you stop criticizing his creation and start thanking him for the way he made you—an important step in learning to accept yourself more and more each day. Once you are released from the prison you've become entrapped in, you will also begin to relate to others in a much more natural and enjoyable way. Your life will gradually become God-centered and other-centered instead of self-centered. Yes, that is one of the paradoxes of self-loathing; it exists in an environment centered on self, even though you do not like yourself.

interesting to note

Many successful comedians once had serious issues with self-acceptance. They've learned that humor is a great resource for overcoming feelings of inadequacy. Stop taking yourself so seriously. Learn to laugh at yourself—not in a demeaning way, but as if you are delightfully amused at the person you have become.

Do you want to stand out? Then step down. Be a servant. If you puff yourself up, you'll get the wind knocked out of you. But if you're content to simply be yourself, your life will count for plenty.
Matthew 23:11–12 MSG

When you take your eyes off yourself and focus instead on God, you will not see all those flaws you are so self-conscious about. And instead of seeing other people through those prison bars, you will begin to see them through the clear lens of God's love.

what's essential

It is important to remember that you are not finished yet. You are not the same person you were a decade ago, and you are not who you will be a decade from now. As you grow in your relationship with God, you will become a better version of yourself. That is something to look forward to—and something you can start working on now.

DO realize that God made you who you are because that is the way he wanted you to be.

DO thank God for who you are, and ask him to help you accept yourself—both the good and what you perceive to be the not-so-good.

DON'T compare yourself with other people, and not just so you will not feel inferior; comparison can have the opposite effect of making you feel superior, which is just as harmful.

DON'T take yourself so seriously; doing so simply intensifies your lack of satisfaction with who you are.

Live Intentionally

You frequently hear people say that you have only one life to live and you should live it to the fullest. They will tell you to get off the treadmill, out of the rut, away from the routine. Live in the moment. Follow your dreams. Ah, if only they would tell you how to do it!

> Do not merely listen to the word, and so deceive yourselves. Do what it says.
>
> **James 1:22** NIV

I t is probably a good thing that some people do not tell you how to live intentionally—to live with a purpose, to stop letting life push you along and start taking control over the course of your life. It is probably a good thing, because unless they include God in the equation, you are going to be miserable trying to find that intentional life without him.

It has been said that once you get to know God, you are forever spoiled for a life without him. You can try to leave him out of some aspects of your life, but sooner or later you will realize it is not worth trying to figure things out without him. So when you begin to live your life intentionally, include God in the process; learn to live intentionally with and for God.

> Faith gives us a focus for our future, helps us move in the direction of our destiny, and gives us the capacity to continue working toward a worthy legacy.
>
> **Mike Huckabee**

Intentional living starts with a purpose, so you already have that covered. Your purpose in life is to love and serve God. That becomes the one thing in your life that motivates everything you do. Your life is intentionally centered on that one thing. Does that mean you have to think about God every minute? Talk about God to everyone you meet? Read only books about God or watch biblical epics on DVD? No. It means that loving and serving God is the driving force in your life, providing a God-centered perspective on everything you do and everything that happens to you in the course of your day.

Passion is the outcome of knowing your purpose and having your picture; now you have to set aside your fears or insecurities to commit to making the picture of what God has given you a reality.
—Randy Carlson

That perspective also enables you to live in the present. Too often, people go through each day thinking about what they are going to do the next day—or regretting what they did the day before. As a result, few people fully experience what is going on at the moment. "Today" barely exists.

Can you see how having a God-centered perspective relates to living intentionally and living in the present? God is not worried at all about tomorrow; his present-moment, here-and-now perspective frees you from worrying about tomorrow and the next day and the next. When you live in the moment, you are free to give your complete attention to the person you are talking to or the situation going on around you or the hummingbird drawing nectar from your window feeder.

Intentional, present-moment living liberates you from more than worrying about the future and regretting the past; it also frees you from such things as envy, because suddenly you realize that the thing you felt so envious about doesn't even fit into your purpose. It helps you discover long-buried gifts and interests that once caused you to dream about your future; when you are no longer distracted by the things that truly do not matter, you are free to discover, or rediscover, the things that bring joy and meaning to your life.

All in all, this is not a bad way to live.

Ephesians 2:10 says this: "We are God's masterpiece. He has created us anew in Christ Jesus, so we can do the good things he planned for us long ago" (NLT). Think about that: you are God's masterpiece, created to do the things he planned for you all along. Do you really believe he created you to run on that treadmill of routine, to stay stuck in the rut that you are mired in? Would he expect that of one of his masterpieces?

interesting to note

One of the benefits of intentional living is that it reduces stress dramatically. When you truly begin to live intentionally in the present moment, it is likely that your breathing will become less shallow, you will feel calmer, and you will begin to take former irritations in stride. You are almost certain to sleep better as well.

Stay clear of silly stories that get dressed up as religion. Exercise daily in God—no spiritual flabbiness, please!
1 Timothy 4:7 MSG

Scottish theologian Carl Bard once made this observation: "Though no one can go back and make a brand-new start, anyone can start from now and make a brand-new ending." You can do that—you really can. Start from now. Start living with purpose. Start living in the present—intentionally. And make a brand-new ending for yourself.

what's essential

 Jesus modeled intentional living throughout his ministry. One example: As the crowd pressed in on him as he was on his way to attend to a dying child, Jesus sensed the touch of one person who needed healing (Luke 8:42–48). The urgency of his mission did not prevent him from responding to an immediate need.

DO learn how to live in the present moment, looking at what is going on right now from God's perspective.

DO make sure that you understand your purpose in living, and center your life on that one thing.

DON'T dwell on the past or worry about the future.

DON'T complicate the process of learning to live intentionally; it is meant to simplify your life, not make it more complex.

How Do I Live My Life Every Day?

GRATITUDE

The LORD is God, and he has shown kindness to us. With branches in your hands, join the feast. Come to the corners of the altar. You are my God, and I will thank you; you are my God, and I will praise your greatness. Thank the LORD because he is good. His love continues forever.

Psalm 118:27–29 NCV

Love wholeheartedly, be surprised, give thanks and praise—then you will discover the fullness of your life.

David Steindl-Rast

In ordinary life we hardly realize that we receive a great deal more than we give, and that it is only with gratitude that life becomes rich.

Dietrich Bonhoeffer